Tuna, Coke & Cigarettes

Tuna, Coke & Cigarettes

A Collection of Atomically Incorrect Stories

Lenny Ricci

Tuna, Coke & Cigarettes: A Collection of Atomically Incorrect Stories
Published by Mufunzarelli Publishing
Aurora, Colorado

Copyright © 2022 by Lenny Ricci

All rights reserved. No part of this book may be reproduced in any form or by any mechanical means, including information storage and retrieval systems, without permission in writing from the publisher/author, except by a reviewer who may quote passages in a review.

All images, logos, quotes and trademarks included in this book are subject to use according to trademark and copyright laws of the United States of America.

ISBN 978-0-578-33505-6
BIOGRAPHY & AUTOBIOGRAPHY / Personal Memoirs

Lenny Ricci
Aurora, CO 80247

Cover Design: Jeff Scott Ruiz, Just Right Publishing
Interior Illustrations: Levi Pike, Redbone Media, levi@redbonemedia.net

For comments, compliments, criticisms or considerations, please email Lenny Ricci at denvrital@gmail.com.

All rights reserved by Lenny Ricci and Mufunzarelli Publishing.
Printed in the United States of America.

Dedication

People often say that they have at least one unforgettable character they remember most in their life. Mine was my good friend, Helen Lopp. Helen worked for me as my secretary when I owned a small TV repair business in New Jersey. She was a shy, quiet, charismatic and very smart old lady who had few words to say; but they were always witty and cutting when she did. Helen made our appointments, answered the phone, did the books and managed all of this while not missing even one minute of several afternoon soap operas that she followed each and every day.

Her lunch routine was manically memorable, so much that I had to use it as the title for this book. Read the story and you'll know why.

To say she had an elephant's memory is an understatement. Helen could master the New York Times Sunday crossword puzzle in less time than it took me to replace a burned-out vacuum tube in a busted television set.

Helen weighed a little less than a sack of spuds; but boy, could she muster up a feisty retort or two when confronted by an unreasonable customer. It was almost like having our very own live-in bulldog.

What I remember and admired most about Helen

is her wit and wisdom. Often, when I would get frustrated while attempting a repair, I would let out a curse word or two. If this went on for more than five minutes, she would quietly get up from her chair, saunter over to me and say something insightful like, "Find your patience before I lose mine."

One day, I confided in her about my sexuality. I was apprehensive at first about letting her in on a very private part of my life, but she was very understanding and supportive. After hearing my story, she sat quietly and nodded a few times. A short while later she said to me, "Always remember, Ricky… you are unique, just like everybody else."

Helen worked for us from day one for over four years, and when the business ended it was difficult to say good-bye. I couldn't have asked for a better friend, confidant and co-worker; and I will never forget her. She wasn't one for much affection, but I did manage to get this photo of her and our postman on the last day of business. Yes, she reluctantly accepted a hug.

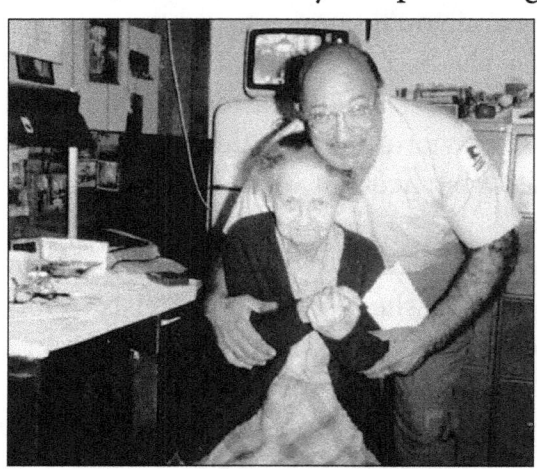

Story Contents

Dedication	v
Foreword	xi
A Child of the City	1
Fireflies and Streetlights	6
Memories of Trains, Uncles and Grandmothers	8
Childhood Antics	13
Christmas Traditions	15
The Lunch Brigade	17
San Berdoo or Bust	19
A Short Stint at RCA	21
Athletics vs. Science	24
The Sunday Nap	28
My Turbulent Teens	30
The Ice Cream Man Cometh	32
The 8-Track Tape Conundrum	34
Framing Nightmares	36
My Italian Angel	39
From Art to Italy	42
The Lucky Mr. Rice	44
The Curse of Amelia	47
PMS, Anyone?	51
Memories of Russ	54
To Tell a Lie	58
Saturday Sex	59
Worst Chocolate Ever	62

The Junk Yard	65
The Good Uncle	70
We Were All Broken Once	73
Cactus Gulch	75
Ahh, Youth!	79
The Rheem Monster	81
Picnicking, Italian Style	84
Father Fanelli's Magic Houdini Box	88
The Italian Evil Eye	91
The Little Fraudsters	94
S&H Green Stamps	98
Nail Clipper Nuisance	101
The Famous Mr. F's Paddle	103
Ah, Ya Mother Wears Combat Boots	107
My Fully Human Self	109
The Sound of Symphony Music	119
I'm Not So Red-Blooded as I Thought	122
My Cat, Max: My Best Friend	125
Dead Lights and Memories	130
Up on the Roof	135
Measles Galore	138
This "Z" Was Not for Zorro	141
See Dick Run	146
Goombas	150
The Re-Ak-Ner	154
Dave and the Thirty Wandering Hens	161
Jenny: The Cat's Meow	167
Tuna, Coke and Cigarettes	170
For 40 Days and 40 Nights	175
For Just a Dollar?	180
The Light Bulb Thief	184
A Visit to the World's Fair	188

My Summer in Carthage	194
The Rain, the Park and Other Things	199
A Great Devilish Adventure	207
A Potato Changed a Life	210
Happiness Isn't Just a Warm Puppy	213
A Slight Distraction	217
The Incident	221
Button Button. Who's Got Yer Button?	226
BOB: An Inspiration. A Remembrance of Max	230
That Red Stuff You Put on Spaghetti	233
I'm a Travelin' Man	235
My Ban-Lon Phase	243
The Bargain Basement	248
Oh, No! Not Another Collection!	253
150 Miracles	259
Discipline	262
Accident Prone	267
The Thomas Crown Roast Affair	271
One Heck of an Ending	276

Foreword

I grew up in what they called the Atomic Age. In the 1950s and 1960s the U.S. was just starting to explore outer space. There was talk about putting a man on the moon. Space capsules, Sputnik and aliens were common dinner conversations, and anything and everything was space related. Oh, and let's not forget about the atom bomb. After the Hiroshima disaster, people were constantly talking about life ending in a ball of nuclear fission. It was always us against them.

I was born in the late 1940s. When I look back at my life, I always thought that I was not put together like most other humans. I always felt that I grew up "atomically incorrect". How else could I explain my weird sense of humor, my many quirks and my enigmatic personality? Teachers would often leave out making comments on my report cards because they failed to truly understand me. Instead, I would get remarks like, "Leonard doesn't try to involve himself with others and prefers to be a loner." That's NOT what a mother wants to hear about her child!

I have a slight suspicion of why I think I am not atomically correct. With all the talk about nuclear explosions and Russia vs. the U.S., our military began experimenting with atomic bombs by dropping them—lots of them—in deserted areas of Nevada. Not even the highest brass in the armed services knew what kind of damage they were doing to the atmosphere or to us humans. They treated radioactivity like it was the common cold. Who knows how much of that radioactive dust I breathed in while playing Kick the Can on Freeman Avenue in Jersey City, New Jersey?

To make matters worse, I became interested in chemistry at the ripe old age of 12. I got my very first A.C. Gilbert introductory chemistry set that year, and I was well on my way to creating my very own atomic explosions in the basement of my parents' home. Shelves were arranged with various Beech-Nut baby food jars that included everything from baking soda to that awful smelling Parson's Ammonia. As a budding chemist, I already knew that everything was made up of atoms, and when unfamiliar atoms are mixed with other unfamiliar atoms, well—reactions occur. I'm sure I breathed in at least a hundred different smelly things that might have messed up my atomic insides.

I hope you get as much enjoyment from reading my life stories as I have had writing about them. At the end of this book, hopefully you will come to understand why I truly feel that I am atomically incorrect. Enjoy!

A Child of the City

I was born in Jersey City, New Jersey, in the summer of 1948. According to the almanac from that year, it was a pretty hot summer. My earliest memories were recorded when I was just a mere tot about two years old. We lived in the middle apartment of a huge four-story building on a small street called Freeman Avenue. Right down the street was Lincoln Park.

My mother would wrap me up like a hoagie sandwich as if it were 22 degrees outside and carry me down the long flight of stairs to the sidewalk outside. Parked next to a ridiculously small patch of dirt with a couple of flowers on it, a lady in a bathtub (I'll explain later), and a chintzy broken-down metal fence, was my baby carriage. Mom stuck me in it and pulled up the large hood to protect me from the glaring afternoon sun. Not to be over-protective, she then laid a fancy hand-knit yellow throw on me and proceeded to push the carriage down the sidewalk toward the park.

The sidewalk was made of large slabs of gray slate, and most of them were broken in two or more places. The spaces between them were raised from nearby roots of the trees planted near the curb. The sound of the wheels hitting every one of those cracks and bumps still echoes in my brain: a soothing sound, a familiar sound that perhaps, if I had been old enough to count, I would remember each and every one to give you a total.

We reached Duncan Avenue and waited for traffic to pass, then made our way into the park. The next thing I heard was kids. Lots of kids. Yelling kids, screaming kids, crying kids. Most of the kids were from the Projects. I didn't quite understand what that meant until I was much older, but I came to realize they were cheap housing units occupied by poor kids whose parents were mostly factory workers, street laborers or domestics. The Project buildings were poorly constructed, and the living spaces were tiny, but the rents were cheap. They were mostly occupied by blacks, Hispanics and many other immigrants. After learning about the Projects, I came to appreciate our huge, but crowded, rooming house.

Freeman Avenue was a microcosm of mixed races. There were Poles, Jews, Chinese, Indians and Italians. You could always tell where the Italians lived because all of them had one or two distinct landmarks in their front yards. One was "Mary in a Bathtub"—that's what we kids called it. It was a statue of the Virgin Mary standing inside of a bathtub-shaped plaster mold. I suppose it was meant to ward off bad spirits, or something like that. Those older Italian mothers and grandmothers held onto many traditions from the motherland.

The other tell-tale sign of an Italian family was a strange looking glass ball, usually silver or blue, that was stuck in the middle of a plaster bird bath. My first thought upon seeing one of them was that it was meant to scare off the birds, rather than attract them to the bath water below. It didn't make much sense to me.

I think I was about six when we finally moved from Jersey City. Dad purchased a rather large ten-room gray house in a sleepy little hamlet called Port Reading. The house had a great big wrap-around front porch with large bay windows, a gigantic incredibly old maple tree in the front yard and a pretty big back yard covered with a thick, plush Kentucky bluegrass lawn.

I don't remember if I had my own bedroom at the time, but bunking with my two younger brothers was a challenge. I was a reader. I loved learning about new things and never tired of reading about far-away places, science things and current events. I was a quiet child. My brothers were loud and mischievous. I needed complete quiet while reading. I hated having to read the same sentence repeatedly because of their chatter, rough-housing and noisily throwing things around.

The only solace I found was in the basement in a little cubby corner next to the coal bin. There was a single 40-watt bulb hanging from the ceiling by its cord and a pull string

that I was just tall enough to reach. I would bring along my *Weekly Reader* school newspaper, my latest copy of *Boys' Life*, and maybe a volume or two of the *Encyclopedia Britannica*. I spent many Saturdays and Sundays down in the basement reading. Once my chores were done, it was my favorite escape from the family. Did I tell you that we had a brood? I was one of nine. I had four older sisters, two younger brothers and two younger sisters.

One of the best things about living in Port Reading was that us kids went to a public school. Back in Jersey City, we were forced to attend Saint Aloysius, a Catholic school where rules could never be broken lest a ruler would come smashing down upon your knuckles. Public school No. 9 was your typical cookie-cutter learning center. We could walk there from home, and most of the teachers were nice compared to the nuns. We still had to attend bible classes. There was no way of getting out of that, I suppose. Mom insisted we learn the Act of Contrition, the Hail Mary and the Lord's Prayer so we could recite them to any aunt or uncle who asked. "It'll cost you at least a nickel or a dime," I would say, and they always gave in. It dawned on me that once I made my First Holy Communion (with lots of money and gifts), I could surely get much more money for repeating a verse or two from a more complicated psalm. It worked for me.

Dad worked a lot. We hardly ever saw him, except for dinner. He had so many different jobs we never knew exactly where our money was coming from. He owned and ran a small gun shop in the tiny town of

Port Reading, and a little further up the road in Carteret he worked in a small pizzeria called the Village Inn. Dad also drove some giant excavation equipment for the New Jersey Turnpike Authority when he wasn't doing anything else. He was good at so many things and he could repair just about anything. Mind you, we didn't have Internet or YouTube back then; you had to learn by doing. A lot of what I know today I attribute to my father.

My dad associated himself with some very unsavory characters. On the few occasions that I got to spend time at the gun shop, I noticed a lot of big burly men in trench coats come and go. Dad would address them by the strangest names, like Guido, Vinnie, Pasquale and Sal. Most of them carried large suitcases and I'm sure they weren't just coming from trumpet lessons. I'll tell you about the poker parties later.

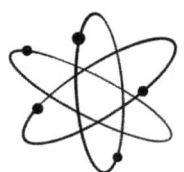

Fireflies and Streetlights

If you ever lived on the east coast, you probably remember catching lightning bugs—or fireflies, as some people called them. Mid-August evenings were the best time to catch the little buggers. It started getting dark around eight, and even though it was close to our bedtime, we would get to stay outside and run around like crazy barefooted madmen with mason jars trying to collect as many as possible. I remember pulling off their little glow lights and sticking them on my fingers and waving them around making patterns in the dark night air. Of course, I was never satisfied unless all ten fingers were adorned.

My bedroom was on the upper floor of our gigantic house. Among other things, I remember summer evenings where I would sit on the corner of my bed near the open window and wait for the streetlight to come on. The light pole was right outside on the edge of our front yard, and it had a green wavy metal reflector on it. Maybe it was a coincidence that the crickets started chirping as soon as the light started to shine on the grass. Sometimes I would see them all hopping around in the wet grass trying to find others of their kind, perhaps to have a cricket party. The chirping sounds were almost hypnotic as you tried to count the seconds in between them.

Staring at that streetlight always made me feel safe. It's not that I was afraid of the dark; but I somehow knew that when the streetlight came on, everything was right with the world—my world.

When it snowed and the front lawn was covered with a smooth silky layer of white, that light would come on; and the wavy lines of that reflector made really interesting patterns in the snow. If the wind was howling, the fixture would jostle back and forth, and the light patterns would be even more mesmerizing. It's funny how little things like light shadows could be so comforting for a kid.

Memories of Trains, Uncles and Grandmothers

My mom had three brothers and one sister. They were all married, and some of the families lived in that huge four-story house on Freeman Avenue. My Uncle Phil lived just two houses down; and my other uncle, Frank, lived about a half mile from there. When we were youngsters, there was no shortage of kids to play with. In the city we had lots of cousins to hang around with, and once we moved to the 'burbs we mostly played with our school chums.

Almost every other Sunday, we would load up the station wagon and make the trek back into Jersey City to visit the family. Sunday dinner was a big deal, but the ride there was the best part of the trip for me. We had an old Country Squire station wagon. Dad would put the rear seats down and place a foam mat in the back. As many kids as he could fit would cram into the car, and away we went.

We would take the New Jersey Turnpike to exit 14B. A railroad track followed the highway for a good 20 miles. I really enjoyed watching and counting the hundreds of oil tank cars that made their way to and from the many refineries along the turnpike. Sometimes, I would get to see the locomotives chugging along, hauling the cars and spewing their smoke into the air and hearing the roar of their engines.

Occasionally, a freight train with lots of different cars would pass and I would be in my glory. For as long as I could remember, I liked trains. Growing up, I had many toy train sets, and they were fun to play with; but seeing the giant rolling stock always gave me a thrill. I could remember naming all the freight lines and their logos: Burlington Northern, B&O, Santa Fe, Great Western, and even the more difficult ones like the Bangor & Aroostook cars. It was like a hobby to me, to try and catalog and remember as many different lines as I could.

Back in the 1960s, telephone lines were strung along the railroad tracks. Sometimes, there might be only two or three wires hanging; but for some long distances there might be eight or more. This may sound strange, but I remember watching those telephone poles and becoming fixated on the sagging wires between the poles. When our car moved along at 50 miles per hour, the poles would whiz by and the wires would sag and tighten at the next pole, and sag again over and over. Watching them would keep me occupied almost the entire length of our trips.

Once we arrived in the city, the adults would meet up and get dinner going. A giant reunion of cousins would begin—running, screaming, playing and having fun. As for me, my first stop was going down to the basement of the house to see my grandmother. My mom's mom, Irene, was one of the kindest, gentlest and most loving adults I knew while growing up. I loved

sitting with her in the kitchen, watching her prepare meals and chatting. She would tell me stories about growing up when she was a little girl, and she shared with me some of her kitchen secrets. Gram loved having me around just as much as I loved being there.

She always wore an apron. It was flowery with two giant pockets. In one of them, she kept a small purple flowery handkerchief that contained a few coins and was neatly tied at the top. After a while, she would pull out that handkerchief, open it up and pull out a nickel or dime. She would grab my hand and press a coin into it, closing my fingers over it ever so tightly and telling me that this was just for me because I was so special. I was never to tell the other kids where the money came from, and I could spend it on anything I wanted.

I learned how to make homemade pasta from my grandmother. She made it seem so easy. Gram had an old metal kitchen table that had hidden side leaves, one on each side. She would open them up, and then wash the table with a bar of ivory soap and a rag. Once dried, she would pour flour in a circle, add some salt and drop whole eggs in the center. She would mix the eggs with the flour a little at a time until a nice dough formed. Then she would knead and knead... and knead some more until she was happy with the texture.

From here, she would form the dough into pasta shapes, sometimes into noodles or ropes, which she cut into small pieces and sometimes just big flat pieces that she dried and used for lasagna. She would sprinkle corn meal on the table and then place the fresh pasta on top of the meal, cover the pasta with light linen towels, then leave them to dry. Sunday dinners in the city were always pasta, salad, antipasto, fresh bread and some sort of meat—meatballs usually, my favorite.

My uncles all smoked cigarettes, except for Uncle Charlie. He smoked those awful smelling stogies. He always reeked of cheap wine and cigars. On top of that, he never gave us kids so much as a hello. My other uncles, on the other hand, would hand us a quarter and tell us to run down to the local corner store and buy them a pack of cigarettes. Back then, they cost 23 cents; but because there was a shortage of copper, the cigarette companies would enclose two pennies in the cellophane and seal it. So, you paid Mr. Bernhardt a quarter for a pack of smokes.

Once we got back to the house, my uncle would open the smokes and hand us the two cents to keep. Of course, right after that, we would high-tail it back to Bernhardt's and spend our fortune on penny candy. If we were thrifty, we could get three orange-flavored candy peanuts for a penny or a whole candy necklace for our two cents, and that lasted almost an entire hour.

Childhood Antics

I got my first cassette tape recorder when I was about 24 years old. Sometime in the mid-70s, small music cassettes took over 8-track players, which were large and bulky, and most of them couldn't record. For as long as I could remember, I liked listening to music from the 30s, 40s and 50s. I would listen to duets by artists such as Frank and Nancy Sinatra, Doris Day and Ella Fitzgerald. Some lyrics were easy to remember, and I loved singing along to tunes on my transistor radio.

With the cassette recorder, I would record my favorite tunes and then entice my sister to help me make a fool of myself. My youngest sister, Maryann, was very much like me. She loved to put on funny skits for family members and act all crazy like some comedians on TV. She and I would do some really funny accents. I could mimic the Germans, and Maryann was really good at mimicking the French. We would team up on occasion and belt out some wonderful duets together.

I remember one in particular: *We're a Couple of Swells*, the original done by Judy Garland and Fred Astaire from the movie, *Easter Parade*. I would turn on the tape recorder and off we would go. Sometimes we would be laughing so hard we'd never get through the first set of lines. Her cheeks would turn beet red from laughing so hard. Later, when I got a portable video tape recorder, we would get even crazier and do some especially fun recreations of movie stars and singers. My best skit was playing Julia Child, complete with my fake French accent. Of course, there would be complete mayhem in the kitchen while I attempted to prepare a fake goose or a gourmet cheese soufflé. I had such fun with Maryann. She could have been the next Carol Burnett.

Christmas Traditions

Most of my memories of Christmas growing up were the same. There would be a 7- or 8-foot real tree (we didn't believe in plastic or aluminum trees) in the corner of the living room, and it would be dwarfed by the biggest mountain of Christmas presents you could imagine. Since we were Catholic, each of the kids had a godmother, a godfather, two sponsors from our first Holy Communion and two more sponsors from our Confirmation.

Every year, we could expect to receive at least six gifts from each of those people, along with other gifts from other aunts and uncles who were just nice and wanted to buy stuff for the Ricci kids. Then there were gifts that each kid bought for our moms and dads and other siblings, and gifts from Mom and Dad to everyone. Now, if you close your eyes, just imagine all of those gifts and where that mountain of gifts originated.

On Christmas Eve, we would invite over friends and family; and sometimes we would celebrate with the Feast of the Seven Fishes. We wouldn't do this every year, but sometimes old traditions won out. This particular celebration originated in southern Italy, and the tradition was that since no meat was to be eaten on the eve of a feast day, seafood was substituted instead.

Why there were seven types of seafood, or eight or eleven, still remains a mystery.

After a hearty meal of clams, salted codfish, mussels in spaghetti, fried calamari, scallops, flounder and smoked whiting, we would then attend Midnight Mass which commemorated the birth of the baby Jesus. As with any Italian celebration, there would be lots of wine, and the drinking would start early and end late. Between all the eating and drinking, there would be clouds of cigar and cigarette smoke hanging in the air throughout the house. Someone would yell and scream to open up some windows, then Dad would yell and scream louder that we're not trying to heat up the entire neighborhood.

Opening up our gifts on Christmas morning usually took about three hours. You can only imagine the pandemonium.

The Lunch Brigade

I was one of four on the infamous Ricci school lunch-making detail. It happened almost every night around 7 o'clock. A large loaf of Wonder Bread would begin the process. One of us would open the bag, take out the slices and arrange them on the kitchen table. Next, the mayonnaise-er would slather the mayo on one slice of bread, and the baloney dealer would lay a slice of bologna on another. The third volunteer in line would plop a slice of yellow American cheese on top of the meat, and then on to the final step of squirting a bit of mustard on the last slice of bread.

One by one, the sandwiches would be placed on wax paper, wrapped and put in a paper bag. Then, we

would take turns adding fruit or a box of raisins, or perhaps a snack bag of potato chips. My older sister, Rene, would write everyone's names on the bag because she had the best penmanship. We had this down to a science and finished the task within a half hour. Good thing, too, because no one wanted to miss any of our favorite tv shows at the time. There would be *To Tell the Truth* on Monday, *Mr. Novak* on Tuesday, *Ozzie and Harriet* on Wednesday, *The Flintstones* on Thursday and *77 Sunset Strip* on Friday. Most of our schoolmates had square metal celebrity-themed lunch boxes. We weren't that lucky, but we were happy to get a decent lunch. We would also get a nickel so we could purchase a half-pint of fresh cold milk to go with it.

San Berdoo or Bust

I started my fledgling college career in San Bernardino, California. I decided to run away from home way back in 1967. My friend, Eddie, and his family were moving from New Jersey to California. Eddie's older sister Pam's husband was taking a job with the San Bernardino sheriff's department and the whole family was moving there for good. They were taking three cars and needed a third driver so they wouldn't have to make any overnight stops; and I agreed to uproot and move there as well.

I looked into enrolling at San Bernardino Jr. College just east of Los Angeles. The school appeared great on paper, and they seemed to have a reasonable tuition rate. It took us four days to travel by car, with some of us sleeping while someone else drove.

We made one major stop at the Grand Canyon because everyone wanted to see it. We parked the van in one of the larger lots and took Eddie's VW to drive around the eastern rim for about 40 miles. It was breathtaking. The clouds over the canyon were moving extremely fast and when the sun filtered through them, they created some incredible effects on the canyon walls. I was lucky to get to see one of nature's most awe-inspiring places and seeing that put the bug in me for future travel.

When we arrived in San Berdoo (as the locals called it), we moved into a rather small house with only three bedrooms. I shared a room with my friend, Eddie. It was small, but we learned to share the confined space without getting in each other's way. I found a job working at Alfie's Fish & Chips, getting paid a whole $3 an hour to cut Icelandic cod. I also worked at a mink farm part time for only a few weeks. The job was easy and fun until I found out that the little critters were being raised to be killed to make mink stoles for the filthy rich of Beverly Hills. I stayed in San Bernardino for two years, got my associate degree and then got homesick for New Jersey and moved back. What was I thinking???

A Short Stint at RCA

I've had a good many different jobs in my lifetime. I'll tell you about the time I worked for the Radio Corporation of America (RCA) in their tube manufacturing plant in Avenel, New Jersey. Way back then, most TVs, radios, stereos and phonographs used electron tubes to power them. Today, of course, we have miniaturized integrated circuits.

My job was to deliver parts to the various workstations around the plant. I had a pushcart and would get requisitions from the various assemblers for the parts they needed to do their jobs in the production of the tubes. I delivered the glass envelopes—the outside of the tube and all the hundreds of small parts that were needed to build the different tubes. I think they made at least 150 different tubes for every kind of job in electronics. Some tubes were the size of a water bottle, and some were no bigger than a thimble.

I really enjoyed that job because I was around machinery, wheels, sprockets and conveyor belts. My fascination for technology was ever-expanding, and I loved watching and learning how it all happened. I had been employed for about six months when, one summer Friday afternoon, I drove into the parking lot to start my 4-11 shift.

As I pulled into a parking space, a motorcycle sped in front of me and decided to take my spot. I had only seconds to react, and… well… I hit the bike, knocked the guy off the bike and ran over his rear tire with my front tire. I was stunned and ran out immediately to see if he was hurt. He was bleeding from the head (they didn't require helmets back then) and he was badly shaken up. There was no time to go into the plant to inform my supervisor of what happened, so I just put the guy in my car and rushed him to the nearest hospital. I felt obligated to stay with him during his emergency room exam and completely forgot to call in to my boss. Roger, the guy I hit, was going to be okay, and they discharged him about four hours later.

We got back into my station wagon and went back to the RCA lot. I picked up his bike and managed to get it into the back of my car. I drove Roger to his apartment and unloaded his bike from my car. I carried him up to his place. I was ridden with guilt, so I stayed with him, made him supper and re-dressed his wounds. The discharge nurse gave me some pills for him, and after dinner I gave him a sedative. I was beat. I then realized it was after 11 pm and I still hadn't called my boss. I checked in with Roger a few times over the weekend by phone and all was good. He was healing with no serious damage (except for the bike).

On Monday afternoon, I drove back into work, pulled my timecard from the rack and saw a note from my boss: "Need to see you in my office ASAP!" I no sooner opened his office door when I got handed a pink slip. "No explanations needed," he said. "A no-show is cause for termination." I was unemployed once again. Sometimes you get whacked for doing the right thing. I wouldn't have it any other way.

Athletics vs. Science

As a kid, I was very shy and reserved. As I mentioned, I loved to read a lot. My two younger brothers were always outside playing. If they weren't playing stickball, they were playing army men. They had sticks fashioned as bayonets and toy plastic guns to shoot the enemy. My brother, Pat, decided to use Dad's folding camping shovel to dig a nice trench in the back yard. He hadn't gotten three feet dug when my oldest sister, Celia, rushed outside to find out what the heck he was up to. "It's a foxhole," he chimed. She demanded he put the dirt back and re-arrange the sod so dad wouldn't find out, or there would be hell to pay.

When I wasn't in my Shangri-La corner of the basement reading, I would sometimes go outside and watch the other kids at play. They were just throwing stones to see who could throw further, and I would just watch and tell myself I could never throw that far; and if I tried and failed, they would just make fun of me. Sure, I wanted to be a part of the crowd; but my meager athletic ability didn't mature until I was a freshman in high school.

I was always thin and frail. In middle school, all the other kids started growing taller. I shrunk. For as long as I could remember, I weighed 125 pounds. Only after a summer of camp did I start to gain a little, but I never did get above five-foot three. At camp, they *made* you swim, run and wrestle; and I did enjoy doing all that stuff, but my passion was still sitting quietly and reading. I managed to get up to 130 pounds in high school and grew to the unbelievable height of five-foot four. My size and weight helped me master the parallel bars, the climbing ropes and the gymnastic rings in gym class; but I would never be able to hit a baseball or tackle a linebacker to save my life.

I remember having to make a model of the earth in science class. The teacher recommended plaster of Paris and newspaper, but we could use anything as long as it came out somewhat earth-looking. We were each

given a round balloon to start with. I rushed home from school and started working on my globe. I asked everyone if we had any plaster of Paris, but nobody knew what that was.

I called my friend, Solomon, because he was the smartest kid I knew. He told me what it was, and just as I thought, we didn't have any. So, I blew up my balloon and started tearing up strips of newspaper soaked in warm water. I had gotten to the part where I needed something to cement all the strips together when I noticed my middle sister, Nora, putting her hair up in curlers. I stopped to watch a few minutes and then asked her what she used to keep her hair in place. She said it was Dippity-do.

After she left the bathroom, I reached into the cupboard and grabbed the jar. It shook like Jello, but was very springy. I ran back into my room and opened the jar. I started smearing the Dippity-do onto the newspaper, and after a few minutes it dried nice and hard. WOW! I thought I found the very solution to keep my globe intact. Before I knew it, I had used up the entire jar. I thought about scotch taping 57 cents to the top of the jar and putting it back in my sister's bathroom, but I decided to be a bit creative.

I had an unopened package of Stripe toothpaste in my bathroom. I took out the box and started to read the label. "Now with Hexachlorophene," it read. I didn't know what that was, but I hoped that it wouldn't be harmful to someone's hair. I opened the box, took out the surprise rocket balloon that came with it, and stashed it in my sock drawer. I twisted the cap off the toothpaste tube and squeezed a little on the counter. It came out red, white and blue. I took the end of the toothbrush and swirled it all together. After blending it, it looked almost the exact color of the Dippity-do: pinkish.

I squeezed every drop of the paste that I could into the now empty jar and swirled it around. It didn't quite feel the same as the hair gel, but I was convinced the girls wouldn't know the difference. I placed the lid back on and put it back into my sister's medicine cabinet. Oddly, I didn't think about it again until about a week later when I heard my sisters talking among themselves, saying how they really liked the mint fragrance they added to the Dippity-do and how much more body it gave to their curls. My lips were sealed. Oh, and by the way, I got an "A" on my science project.

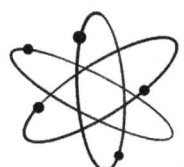

The Sunday Nap

Our dad, for some strange reason, loved to take a nap on the living room rug on Sunday afternoons. He would set up the giant metal box fan, put it on medium about two feet away, lay an old comforter and a couple of pillows down and take a snooze. The bad thing was that he always insisted that his three sons join him. I guess that was his way of bonding with us. However, it seemed like punishment to us.

Sundays were our days off from school, and when we weren't doing homework, we enjoyed playing and doing our own things. Dad would do this really loud whistle with two of his middle fingers and we would have to come running. With frowns of despair, we would lie down beside him and take a nap. The good thing was that it would take him about ten minutes to be snoring away. We knew that once he started snoring we could get up, sneak off, and he'd never be the wiser. Usually, it worked.

One Sunday, after settling in for his nap, we had a power outage. The fan stopped working and dad woke right up. He noticed that the three boys had gone AWOL, so he summoned us again with his whistle. I was in the basement and my brothers were probably down the street playing with the neighbor kids. After hearing the whistle, I snuck back upstairs and peered into the living room. My brothers weren't there, so I decided it was best that I stay in hiding, too.

As it turned out, dad was no longer interested in napping, but was going to take all the kids out to the Dairy Queen for ice cream. He gathered all who were around, and they got into the station wagon and left. We boys were left at home, and I cursed the electric company.

My Turbulent Teens

It's often said that the middle child in a family has a natural knack to negotiate. Middle kids grow up to be political diplomats, mediators and go-betweens. The reason for this is simple: they have always had to resolve conflicts between their older and younger siblings. I was a middle child. Negotiating my place in the hierarchy of the family was difficult. I was forever being told, "You are the oldest of the young'uns, and you should know better." Sure, I was older; but when it came to me being responsible, I was just as reckless at times as my younger siblings were. I always tried to push the envelope and see how much I could get away with.

When I got older and my five elder sisters moved out of the house, I was the only one left who had a driver's license. Suddenly, I was the one everyone depended on to drive them to the mall, to school, to grocery shopping, etc. Suddenly, I felt needed. Many a Sunday would arrive when Mom suggested I treat her to a ride in the country. Of course, I would agree, then everyone who was going would scurry around gathering this and that; and finally, when everybody was ready, I would snidely say I wasn't interested in going any more. Oh my God, my mother would start ranting and raving because I changed my mind. I'm not sure why I did that, but I did it a lot. I guess it was because they all were manipulating me, and I felt that I had lost control. I think I gave in at least once or twice after pulling that stunt. If I were my mother, I would have given me away to the gypsies.

The Ice Cream Man Cometh

There were three competing ice cream trucks that used to come around on summer weeknights and weekends in our neighborhood. The more unfamiliar ones were the Freezer Fresh trucks. Next was Mr. Softee; and my favorite one was Good Humor. On hot summer nights we would often hear the faint jingle of the bells of the Good Humor truck. All the kids within earshot would listen as the sound got louder and louder, meaning the truck was right around the corner of East Richard Street and Mason Drive. The driver always knew he would gather a nice little crowd of scroungy looking bare-footed kids with at least a dime to spend. He would park between our house and Mrs. Hurley's. There were no rules to follow about who

got to go first. There was, however, minor chaos and mayhem. The ice cream man would get out of his cab and come around to the side of the truck, and the first dime that was waved in his face got his attention.

Depending on how much money I had, I would choose the cheaper banana Fudgsicle or my all-time favorite, strawberry shortcake. My brothers always got the Big-Top, a vanilla and chocolate ice cream cone dipped in melted chocolate and dipped in crushed peanuts. My sister, Nora, loved the plain chocolate Fudgsicle; and my younger sister, Judy, chose the plain old half-vanilla, half-chocolate cup with a wooden spoon. If Mr. Softee got there before the Good Humor guy, the choices were narrowed down to three—vanilla soft, chocolate soft or a swirl of half-and-half. They had good ice cream, but it never satisfied my taste for my strawberry shortcake. The third guy, Freezer Fresh, also had a nice variety of different ice creams, but the quality wasn't as good as Good Humor. He did have one thing the others didn't: a frozen banana dipped in melted chocolate, and it was pretty reasonable for a nickel. Nowadays, we still have a truck roaming our neighborhood from time to time; but they now play an annoying little ditty that you can't get out of your head. I'm sure the kids don't mind; but for an adult, it's just plain irritating.

The 8-Track Tape Conundrum

Before the invention of the audio cassette, there were 8-track tapes. For anyone not familiar, it's an enclosed loop of recording tape in a cartridge with one rubber wheel used to transport the tape across a playback head. The tape goes back into the center of the reel and runs continuously until stopped. 8-track tapes were very convenient for car tape systems because you could play your favorite music for over an hour, then pop in another one in seconds while driving.

I remember one of my favorite 8-tracks was the group, The Four Seasons. I could listen to their version of *Sherry* over and over again. One evening, I was lying on my bed and my 8-track player was hooked up to my rather inexpensive JC Penney stereo system. At full volume you could almost hear the music above the sound of my small box fan. I laid there waiting for my favorite tune to come on and relaxed with my eyes closed. When it was over, I went over to the stereo to pull out the tape, and to my surprise the tape had unwound itself. Yards and yards of milk chocolate-colored, ribbon-like tape was all over the floor! I was in a panic because I didn't know how to fix it. I opened the small trap door and pulled the cartridge out a bit. It stopped playing, and I pulled it out a little more.

Bunches of wrinkled tape were all over the inside of the mechanism. I gently pulled out more and more of the tangled tape and finally got it all out. *Damn*, I thought to myself. How am I going to fix this mess? I got out my pocketknife and sliced into the label holding the two halves together. I pried the two halves apart and looked inside. In the center was the large reel. I took it out and laid it on a table, and ever so gently started winding the messed-up tape back onto the reel. This took about 2 hours, but I was determined. I smoothed out all the wrinkles of every inch of tape, and I wrapped and wrapped until it was back to normal. I popped it back into the holder and snapped the two pieces together. Now for the moment of truth. I popped it back into the player and it started playing again— for about 35 seconds. It started playing, *Ain't That a Shame*. Then the sound got muffled; and it sounded like an old Victrola record player when the cranked spring ran out. The tape started spewing back out of the machine and onto the floor again. How ironic that it picked *that* final song to conk out on. Yep, that was a shame!

Lenny Ricci

Framing Nightmares

One of my many vocations was that of a CPF. No, that doesn't stand for Certified Public Financier. I was a picture framer. I got my degree from a company called Larson-Jule. This company was one of the largest suppliers of art and framing supplies in the US, and I was certified way back in 1998. I worked as a framer for a few companies like Ben Franklin, Frank's Nursery and Crafts, and a bigger company called Michael's Stores. I framed the run of the mill things like prints, photographs and posters. I then started working for a company that let the customer help out in the framing, aptly called Frame It Yourself.

Since I lived in Denver, I framed a lot of Denver Broncos memorabilia, as well as Colorado Avalanche items. After a while, framing jerseys, trading cards, helmets and hockey pucks got boring. I started learning how to shadow box. Once I became good at it, we started advertising; and next thing I knew, I was framing some of the most unusual stuff you could imagine.

One middle-aged woman with deep shades of rouge on her cheeks came in and said she wanted her nails framed. I asked what she had in mind, and she spread her tiny hands out to me with 4-inch long delicately painted nails. "These!" she said. I was a bit perplexed, as they were still attached to her fingers. After getting my approval that I could frame them, she took out a large pair of wire snips and off they came. I gently picked them up with a Kleenex and put them into a plastic bag, wrote up her order, then she left.

My next oddity came from a gentleman of about fifty. He was gray-haired and with a beard to match. He was dressed in khaki pants and a camo T-shirt. "What can I help you with, sir?" I asked. "I would like you to frame my war souvenir," he said. With that, he opened up an oblong metal box and took out a very long and skinny piece of ragged metal. "This shrapnel was stuck in my leg for a good week while I was in 'Nam." I looked a little closer and noticed there was a nice coating of dried blood and small patches of dried-up skin on it. "Do you want me to clean it up first?" I asked. "Nope! Just stick it in a box along with this photo of me in the medic ward and my Medal of Valor next to it."

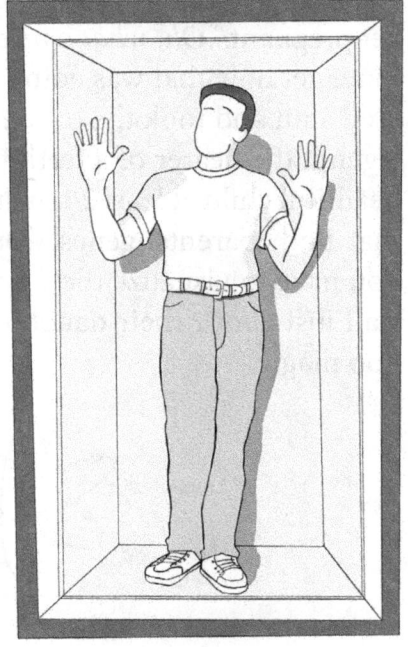

"How long has it been in this box?" I asked. "Oh, about 35 years," he said. I was a little concerned about that blood developing some kind of mold being sealed behind glass, so I told him I would have to spray it with some acrylic spray beforehand. "Nope," he said, "I'll take my chances. I want everyone to see my splattered blood and guts very clearly." 'Nuff said.

Finally, I had a nice middle-aged couple come in all dressed up like they were going to the opera. The woman had white pearls around her neck and the man wore a yellow kerchief around his. They were very tall and dapper people. He opened a shopping bag and pulled out a fancy box with some strange writing on it. It looked like Hindu, but I wasn't sure. Inside, nestled in a light purple cocoon of silk material, were 2 miniature dolls. I just stood there and waited for their story. "They are fertility dolls," he said. "They are from the jungles of Borneo, and they are very sacred." We want to give them to our oldest daughter so she can get pregnant." *Oh, what a nice gift*, I thought. I couldn't quite get how that was going to work, but I just snickered a bit and took the order. According to an African legend, the bearer of a fertility doll will give birth to a beautiful child at least 24 inches tall. I personally think that both parents' genes would have done the trick. You have to visualize the framed dolls hanging on the wall just above their daughter's bed doing their Voodoo magic.

My Italian Angel

One beautiful Sunday afternoon, I decided to take a drive to see my grandmother in Jersey City. I lived in a small town on the Jersey shore about 25 miles south. I got in my giant '66 Chevy Chevelle station wagon and headed for the New Jersey Turnpike. It was a pretty cloudless sky, and the afternoon sun was warm and inviting. I rolled down my windows and began my trek. I had gotten about five miles when I noticed a pretty large flatbed truck about a quarter mile ahead in the right lane. It had what looked like metal barrels stacked on each other and they were all secured with very wide red canvas straps. I was in the middle lane, a good distance behind the truck, listening to some oldies on the radio and feeling the warm breeze on my arm and face. There were two cars coming up alongside of me, one on the left and one on the right.

All of a sudden, the truck decided to abruptly veer into the middle lane, which caused his trailer to tilt to the left off one of its rear wheels. What I saw next was frightening. One of the canvas load ties snapped and the barrels started to roll off the back of the truck. As they hit the concrete pavement, they sparked and started rolling towards me. I panicked. As I looked in both side mirrors, I saw the two other cars were right alongside me, which prevented me from changing lanes. I peered into the rear-view mirror, and luckily there was no one behind me for a good distance.

I quickly slammed on my brakes and slowed down just enough to cut the wheel to the right and go off onto the shoulder. Two of the barrels rushed past me, tumbling and turning, and they finally got stuck in the center metal barrier. I sat in my car trembling for what seemed like an hour. I saw that the flatbed driver had pulled over way up ahead and he was walking towards my car. All I could hear was my heart racing and the drone of my directional blinker pinging and pinging. My eyes were fixated and blank. I reached up to feel my forehead. I was sweating profusely. The driver finally came up to my window and asked about me. "Thank God you got out of the way," he said. "Those barrels were filled with liquid petroleum, and God only knows

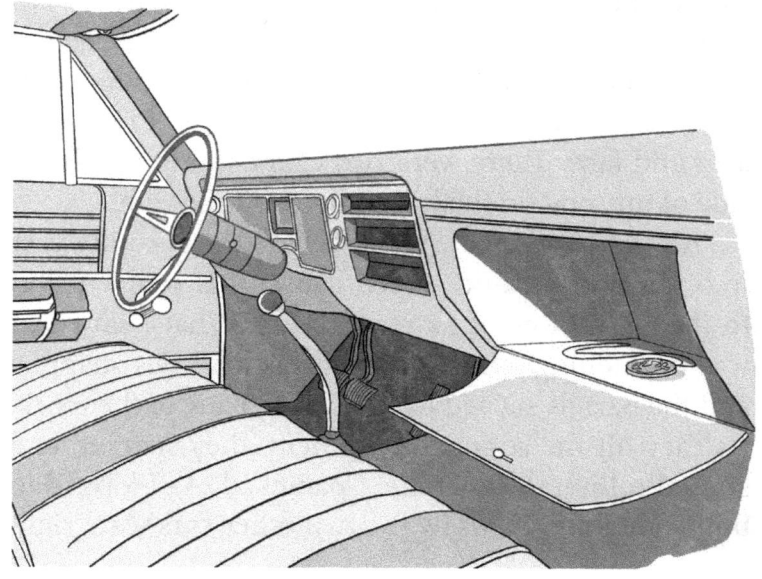

what would have happened if one of them hit your car. "You are a very lucky young man." I couldn't speak just yet, so I just nodded. He walked back to his truck and secured the rest of his cargo, then got on his CB radio to hopefully call the police and report the incident. It took me at least a half hour before I was calm enough to continue my trip.

Once I arrived at my grandmother's and told her what had happened, she sat me down and told me she had a premonition that something was wrong and had gone to her jewelry box to get her Saint Christopher medal. Saint Christopher is the patron saint of travel. Even though my grandmother didn't drive, she—like a lot of older Italian women—retained a good-sized collection of various saint medallions meant to protect their loved ones from harm and danger in most any situation. Gram told me that when she put it in her hand and closed her fist it seemed to glow ever so slightly, and she felt a wave of relief. This must have happened just when my almost fatal highway catastrophe was happening. Gram turned to me, opened my hand and pressed the charm into it. "Put this in your glove box," she said. St. Christopher just may have saved my life that fateful day; and when I sold the car years later, the charm went with it. I hope it found a new human to protect.

From Art to Italy

In 2004, the citizens of Denver passed a vote providing funds to build an addition onto the existing Denver Art Museum. The multi-million-dollar addition was designed by famed architect, Daniel Libeskind. The city was very excited to see the expansion happen, and hopefully it would bring lots of tourist dollars to Denver. Work on the Hamilton building began in late 2004, and they started hiring new staff for the facility in January of 2006. I, along with about six other salaried employees, took a tour of the building in February and I started working as merchandise coordinator in March.

My job was basically to assist the museum's gift shop buyer by installing displays, stocking and maintaining the warehouse, and receiving merchandise from many different vendors. I was in charge of the warehouse which was located in the basement of the new building. I had about 30 employees, mostly in their 30's; but some older seniors also worked there strictly as greeters and stock persons. I loved working there and I got to use my head along with my muscles. Some days there would be up to 50 deliveries—everything from books to glassware, and umbrellas to music CDs. The buyer was a bit of a tyrant, demanding at times more than what my crew and I could provide; but we got along, and things went smoothly. I also loved the money. I was making more money there than I had ever made in my entire life. I got to use my creativity in creating unique holiday displays, and on special occasions I would get to add my two cents as to what new items to bring in. I honestly never thought I would leave that job. After the first year of the opening of the new Hamilton wing, attendance dropped off tremendously and there were rumors that we would have to cut back our hours. When the word came down from the board of directors, we were certain there would be layoffs. I never expected to be one of them.

In July of 2007, I resigned my position and accepted a really good severance package and bonus pay. I was devastated from losing this job, but life goes on. I decided to take the nice fat check and travel to Italy, spending a good three weeks traveling by train to a dozen or more cities. I had the grandest time. When I got back in October, I picked up the Sunday *Rocky Mountain News* and found an ad for a company looking for a person to do electrical repairs working on German-made vacuum cleaners. Long story short—out of the dozens who applied, I got a job as Tech Manager. I've been there about 14 years now and I just love it. From art to dirt… now, that's a switch.

The Lucky Mr. Rice

The laws of physics say that no two automobiles can occupy the same space at the same time. I had no intention of proving that theory when I plowed into the front left side of a pickup truck that ran a red light. This was before air bags and seat belts were becoming popular in passenger cars. My car was a tank. It was a 1967 Pontiac LaSabre, dark navy blue with light blue interior. The front bumper was fashioned like a steel beam and just as strong. My car weighed about half a ton. The pickup was one of those new-fangled rice burners imported from Japan. They called it a Datsun 620, and it weighed as much as a tiny 78-year-old grandmother soaking wet. It's no wonder that when I smashed into it, the lightweight toy car careened out of the intersection, spun around like a yo-yo and landed on the grassy embankment nearby. My destroyer of a car suffered a little chrome paint loss and maybe a little remorse.

I pulled over to the truck and got out of my car. The lone driver, a middle-aged man of 50 or so, opened his door and sauntered out. He seemed okay, but was in a bit of a daze from being tossed around like a stuffed cat toy smacked by an overweight tabby. We chatted a bit and exchanged phone numbers. His car was still drivable, and we decided there was no sense getting the local police involved. Without so much as a bruised finger on either one of us, we parted ways.

About three weeks later, I got a letter from an insurance company lawyer. I thought it might have been a letter saying all was good, but then I looked at the first line of the letter: *You are hereby being sued by...* WOW! I was being sued by his insurance company for causing an accident and apparently it was my car that went through the light, not his. Of course, there were no witnesses or street cameras, and no one had cell phones back then; so, it was my word against his. I panicked for about ten minutes, cursed a few choice words and slammed my palm down on the kitchen table. My sister, Nora, was nearby and came in to see what the matter was. I showed her the letter

and she looked briefly at the heading. I put my head in my hands and sulked. "This isn't you," she said. "It's addressed to a LEO-NAIDE C. RICE," she said.

I grabbed the letter and looked at it again. Sure enough, it was addressed to a Mr. Leo-naide C. Rice—not to Leonard G. Ricci. "Someone made a big mistake," she said. I called the lawyer right away and thankfully got that mess straightened out. About a week after that, I got a check in the mail for $42.65 made out to the real Leonard Ricci. I lived with the chrome paint defect and brought myself some new seat covers for my beast.

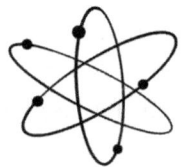

The Curse of Amelia

I don't believe in too many superstitions. I have no problem with walking under a ladder or crossing the path of a black cat. Sometimes, I even step on cracks in the sidewalk, knowing that since my mom is no longer living, she could not develop back trouble. In Germany, they say if you toast a cheer while drinking water, you are actually wishing death on the person you are toasting with. The Japanese think that if you sleep with your head facing north, the following day you will have bad luck because that is how the deceased are laid to rest. I also don't believe that if a bird poops on you it begets good fortune. I've had three seagulls poop on me and all I got was a hefty dry-cleaning bill. There is, however, one unjustified belief I have in the supernatural that I cannot deny: the curse of Amelia. Let me explain.

My mom used to work as a housekeeper in a nursing home called Arnold Walters. She worked in the women's section. Basically, she did a bit of light cleaning and gave the ladies help with bathing, changing clothes and just making their lives a little more tolerable. There was a community room where they gathered to play cards, knit, converse and sing. There was a piano in the room, but none of the residents could play more than a few notes. One day, Mom was talking with a few ladies and mentioned that I could play the piano. She tried to persuade me to come in and play some tunes. I was reluctant at first, but after mom explained that these old people didn't have much time left and were just existing in their rooms, I decided to visit on a Saturday afternoon.

All the ladies were excited to see me, and one by one they asked me if I knew this tune or that tune. Most of the songs they wanted were old tunes from the 1940s; and I knew quite a few of them because mom used to play her old 78 RPM records over and over while I was growing up. I picked up a lot of the tunes just by repetition. I had taken about eight requests, and then after a short rendition of *Drink to Me Only with Thine Eyes*, I got up and started to say my good-byes. Just then, a woman named Amelia got up, came over to me and asked me to play her favorite song, *Lady of Spain*. She pleaded with me and finally I said to her that I was sorry I didn't know that tune. She started humming it, but I still didn't know it. As I started to leave, she pleaded with me again and this time she was beginning to get nasty. "Young man," she shouted, "You'd better play my song or else."

WOW, I thought! She is really feisty. Once again, I told her that I didn't know *Lady of Spain*, and I started walking out. Amelia wasn't accepting NO for an answer. She told me she was going to put a curse on me and my entire family. "Strange things will happen to you," she said. "Mark my words! You will be haunted by me until you die!" she shouted. I was already halfway out the door when I looked back to see Amelia holding up one hand with her pinky and pointing finger standing straight out and directing it towards me. I couldn't get away from that place any faster.

I didn't give much thought to Amelia for years. One day, later on, I was living in St. Petersburg, Florida with Jimmy. We had just had a really nice afternoon thunderstorm. The temperature had dropped enough that we decided to turn off the air conditioner and turn on a fan to bring some cool air into the house. I went over to the window A/C and switched it off. It kept running. I turned the switch a few more times, and it still kept running. I pulled the plug from the wall out-

let, and it still kept running. I yelled for Jimmy to come over and we both stood there in awe. "How could that be?" I said. "It doesn't make any logical sense." About a minute later it stopped. We both looked at each other and said her name.

Over the years we have had numerous electrical issues in our homes, and each and every time we both thought that it must be Amelia. We may never really know how or why those things occurred, but I can't help believing that she somehow played a role in our supernatural electrical mishaps. We never mentioned or said her name out loud from then on. We even avoided answering a question on Jeopardy that mentioned the lady aviator who disappeared while flying solo across the ocean.

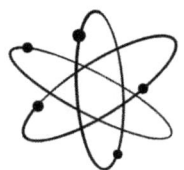

PMS, Anyone?

If you grew up with older sisters, you found out rather quickly about "the monthly curse." My four older sisters were subject to this dreaded monthly occurrence, and each one visited a different kind of hell on everyone else in the family. Because there were four different women with four different cycles, the hysteria and pandemonium never ended. My brothers and I never knew if their actions from one moment to the next were rational or being dictated by their wacko hormones. The mood swings were the worst. One minute, the enemies would be talking about taking you out for an ice cream soda, and the very next minute they were banging your head against the wall for allowing a spider to get onto the living room couch.

My second-oldest sister, Rennie, once chased me around the living room, through the kitchen, into the hallway and back, and through the living room again three whole times before I eluded her by opening up the basement door and escaping down the stairs. As I reached the bottom, she unhooked a rather large frying pan from the side wall and flung it like a discus at my head. CLUNK. It hit me on the back of my head, and I was down. Luckily, I have a thick skull and there was no permanent damage done, other than a nice knot which I still wear to this day. My fourth-oldest sister, Nora, would binge eat to help ease her emotional rollercoaster. Her time of the month included extra helpings of sad and heart-wrenching emotions that could only be dissolved by eating an entire Sara Lee cheesecake and watching back-to-back reruns of *Little House on the Prairie*. With a box of tissues and her 9" black-and-white Sony portable TV, her mornings would melt into afternoons and gradually slide into evenings.

The depression would fade only after 6:00 pm, when her husband and kids would appear and get restless for their supper. She would manage to defrost some chicken nuggets, re-heat some whipped potatoes from the previous night's dinner and wrangle up a can of Green Giant corn. After throwing the food on some cheap plates, doling out some mismatched forks, she would then retreat to the back yard with her Sony

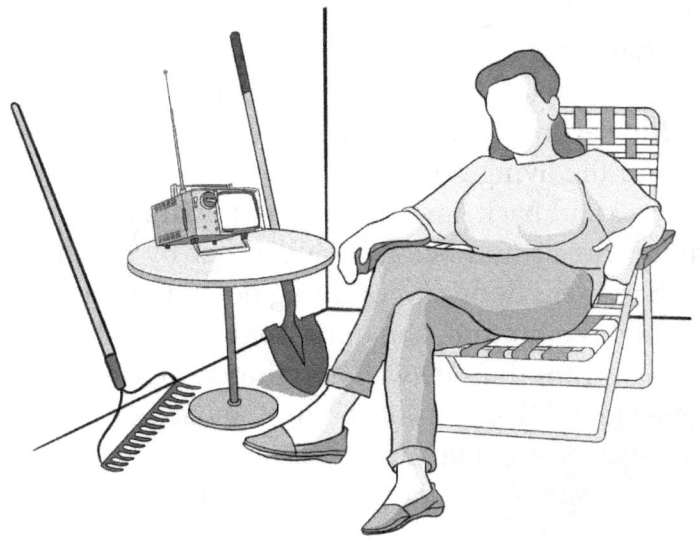

TV, where she would sit in a corner of the shed and bawl uncontrollably. After 15 or so minutes, Andy, her husband, would seek her out and try to get an explanation. "There's no one in the shed who will judge me," she would say. That was Andy's clue to leave the PMS alone and seek higher ground. Twenty minutes later she would be back in the kitchen wearing a cheery flowered apron, dancing to some oldies and cleaning up the kitchen.

Life was once again tolerable.

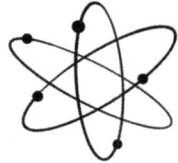

Memories of Russ

The good thing about being a 16-year-old skinny teenager was that I could run fast. I was awful at sports, unlike my two brothers. I couldn't catch a pass on a football field if it were painted florescent red and had a homing device attached. I couldn't sink a basketball if I had stood on a ladder and plopped it in from three inches away.

I excelled in gymnastics. I was really good on the pommel horse. I could climb up a rope faster than most of my gym class buddies, and I could spin and twirl on a set of rings faster than half of those other boys. I loved to run. We had a regulation-sized track at Raritan High, and I practiced almost every chance I got. I tried out for cross country and made the team.

During my junior year, we competed against some of the best high school teams in neighboring schools, and we took home many winning trophies. I continued track and field into my senior year. Aside from track, I had joined the radio club that year and made a few close friends through our mutual interest in the sciences. One senior, Russ, and I became good friends. We had chemistry class together and we were also lab partners. I didn't make too many really close friends, as most everyone there considered me a nerd and a square. Russ was very athletic, and he tried out for just about every sport. His main passion was for running, just like mine. We practiced, sprinted against each other and we often did relays together. Our last period class was gym, and we would often finish class and go out and run some laps.

One particular afternoon in late May we were out on the field. We had just finished the circuit and were nearing the finish when I spotted lightning in the distance. I could see storm clouds approaching, and as Russell rounded the corner, I yelled at him to come in and pointed to the developing storm. He glanced to the west and slowed down just long enough to tell me that he wanted to go around one last time. As he passed me, I yelled again. "Russ, please stop now, get back here." He ignored me, and within a minute it started to pour. The coach then raced out onto the grounds and demanded that everyone get inside. He walked up to the metal entrance gate, shut it and ushered us all into the dug-out.

The storm was intensifying, and bolts of lightning were striking every few seconds. I shouted to the coach that Russ was still on the field, and he told me to just stay put and not go out there. "I'm sure he knows what to do in a thunderstorm," he said. I stood by that door getting pounded by heavy drops of rain, and with every strike of lightning I tried to make sight of my friend. It was coming down so hard that I could barely see a foot in front of me.

The rolling blasts of thunder and the intense cracks of lightning kept me from moving, but my concern for

Russell's welfare overshadowed my own safety concerns. I pulled a towel off of a nearby rack and covered my head. I ran out onto the field toward the track, and I spotted Russ heading for the gate. Thank God, I thought! Russ noticed that the gate was closed, so he decided to just climb over the fence and high-tail it back.

He no sooner grabbed onto the top of the metal fence when lightning struck his head. I saw the whole thing. I watched the bolt strike him and he froze in position like a statue of a Greek god. Time seemed to slow down, and everything went into slow motion. The electric charge turned from hot white to pink. Little threads of plasma trickled from his body to the fence and disappeared into the ground.

I was in shock as I dropped to the ground and dug my hands into the muddy earth. I reached up to pull the towel from my eyes and watched as Russ's clasped hands released their grip on the fence and he fell. By this time, the coach, who had been standing by the door of the dug-out, rushed outside and ran to my side. He picked me up and asked me if I was all right. All I could do was mutter some incoherent words as he carried me inside.

By the time an ambulance arrived, Russell was dead. In just a brief moment his life was cut short. His future career as a research chemist was erased. Graduation was just three weeks away, and Russell wouldn't be there to receive any honors.

It took me many months of talking with school counselors and mental health advisers to finally be at peace with what I saw. I still have great memories of Russ, and I often think of the commemorative plaque that hung in the hallway of Raritan High:

> "Russell… To Live in Hearts We Leave Behind Is Not to Die" —*Thomas Campbell.*

To Tell a Lie

When I was seven years old, my sister, Kathy, took me and my other sister, Lenora, to see *Pinocchio*. It was playing at the State Theatre on Main Street in Woodbridge. As I recollect, it was the first Disney movie I saw in a movie house. I was impressed by the large screen and loudspeakers. The scene where the whale spits out Geppetto and Pinocchio as they get washed ashore in a huge wave was extremely loud and memorable. But what was more memorable was the first time I lied after seeing that movie. For weeks after, I began touching my nose every time I told a fib. At first nobody noticed, but after a while people kept asking me if I had a sore nose. I'm sure the people at Disney knew this story would cause some young impressionable minds to be good and to do right by others. But whatever you do, don't squash any crickets, for those bugs just might be your subconscious speaking.

Saturday Sex

Another of my short-lived careers was working as a manager in the Lawn and Garden Center of Frank's Nursery & Crafts in St. Petersburg, Florida. My job was pretty simple—manage a small crew, order and receive plants and garden equipment and take care of inventory. I loved working with plants, getting to know different varieties of fauna and flora, and best of all, being outside most of the day. Although my thumb was mostly beige, I was blessed with a staff of knowledgeable people who did in fact have green ones.

Some of my employees were part-timers who worked after school and on weekends, and some were temps who just wanted to make extra spending money. I depended mostly on my full-timers. Most of them were very dedicated and willing to put in a good day's work— except for Conchita. Conchita was a youngish middle-aged woman of Mexican descent. Her English was fairly good, she was quite talented, and she was a conscientious worker. When I hired her, I asked if working nights or weekends would be an issue; and she replied that she needed all the hours she could get, so it wouldn't be a problem.

After about six months, she changed her tune. I posted the schedule for the following week, and since

we were going to have a special spring flower sale, I needed all of the staff to work the weekend. Conchita glanced at the schedule posted on the break room wall and came storming into my office to complain. "I can't work Saturday evening," she said in her best broken English. I asked her if there was a reason, and she said she just couldn't, and that I should get someone else to fill her slot. I again asked her what the reason was and reminded her of our oral agreement about weekend work back when she was hired. "My husband has different hours now," she said.

"And how does that affect YOUR job, Conchita?" I asked back. "Well, Saturday night we… You know… we do it!" she said. "Do what?" I chimed in. "Well, we just do it on Saturday," she barked. Again, I demanded to know what she was talking about. "Do you play Bingo with friends? Do you and your husband go bowling? Is that the night you cut each other's toenails?"

That third one got to her, and she started jabbering on in Spanish. There were a lot of words I didn't know, and with each breath she took, her Spanish got louder and meaner. Finally, she leaned over to me and whispered in my ear. "Saturday is the only night we *tenemos sexo*. "Oh," I gasped. I finally got it! After thinking of what she said, I suggested a few things. "Do you know what saltpeter is?" I asked. "No!" she answered. "How about cold showers?" I asked. She didn't quite understand that one, either; and I wasn't about to give her a lecture on male hormones.

Finally, I tried to reason with her. "I need you here on Saturday nights because you are the best person I have to watch over all the other flunkies." She asked, "What is flunkies?" I answered, "Well, those are people who are not dedicated like you. Those are people whom I cannot trust to do all those little things that you do so well and make me proud. Those are the types of people who will not be getting a nice big fat raise when I do reviews," I commented. "Oh, Mr. Lenny", she blurted. "I think my husband and I can work out other day to do boom-boom. I replied, "I knew you could work something out, Conchita. Gracias."

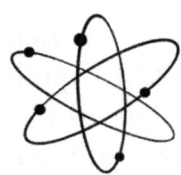

Worst Chocolate Ever

I'm not sure why I was so fascinated with other people's medicine cabinets, but I was. Whenever we visited any of our relatives' homes, I would always manage to sneak a peek into their medicine chests. I would always make sure the bathroom door was locked because I didn't want anyone coming in while I was snooping through all their medical stuff. Some of my aunts kept the strangest things in there. My Aunt Louise's cabinet was really full of lots of interesting things. Among the bottles of pills were the usual things, like those cute little bottles of blood red Tincture of Mercurochrome and the distinct blue bottle of Milk of Magnesia. One time, I found a small, flat foil pouch about the size of a pocket tin of Bayer aspirin tablets. Of course, being only seven or eight years old, I had no idea what a prophylactic was, and I could hardly even pronounce the word. I stuck it in my pocket to explore later. There was another small blue box stuffed behind a jar of English Leather cologne. I opened the box and immediately smelled the contents. "Hmmm, chocolate," I thought. Who would put a box of chocolate in a medicine chest? I pulled out a sleeve of the foil-lined candy and opened it. There were eight very tiny pieces of chocolate all separated like a full-sized

Hershey bar, except that instead of an "H" and an "E" and an "R", they were marked with the letters "EX" and "LAX". Since I never heard of that brand before, I pondered on whether to eat just one or be a glutton and consume the whole thing right there and then. I did the latter. When we arrived back home from my aunt's house, I started feeling strange. My stomach was gurgling and I was nauseated. I was almost doubled over when Mom noticed my erratic behavior. "What's wrong?" she asked. I couldn't tell her I had eaten all of my aunt's chocolate, so I just told her I didn't feel well. With that, she pushed on my tummy and immediately picked me up and sat me down on the throne. You can guess what happened next. The next couple of days were spent in and out of the bathroom, and I decided never to eat anything that came out of anyone's medicine chest ever again. Oh… the condom wound up floating like a balloon in the washer a few days later, and no one said a word.

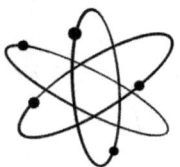

The Junk Yard

I loved exploring. My brother-in-law, Skip's, family owned an auto salvage yard in Toms River, NJ, and it had been in the family for perhaps 60 or so years. The junk yard was huge. It must have been at least 200 or 300 acres with junk cars dating from way back in the 1930's. I loved to wander into the graveyard of old cars, some overgrown with plants and trees and rusted beyond recognition.

On the days I knew I was going exploring, I would wear a pair of old ripped up overalls and a tee shirt, as the insides of some of these old wrecks were just filthy and filled with who knows what kinds of deadly germs. I didn't know one car model year from another, so I just looked for cars that caught my eye. As I walked deeper into the vast cavern of abandoned cars, I started to wonder how and why some of these vehicles wound up here. Some cars were definitely in accidents; but some were intact and just old—probably with blown engines or transmissions—and were forced to come here because the owners could not afford to fix them.

I wondered about others. I would see an old giant Buick, then climb into the back seat and imagine who sat here before me. I sometimes searched under the seat cushions for old coins and other interesting things. I once came across a baby bottle and bib, and wondered if that little human lost its life in that car. Across the path lay an old camper, its front smashed in like an accordion. I opened the back door, and inside I found a fully decorated Christmas tree lying on its side with many of the ornaments broken and still hanging on by tiny threads. On the small counter was a gift box with the remains of what once was a pretty red ribbon. I turned over the tag and it read, *To my darling Clarice… Merry Christmas.* My mind wondered whether or not Clarice ever got to celebrate that Christmas.

An old Studebaker sedan beckoned me next. It had strange, curved and separated front windshields and the doors both opened from the center. The inside upholstery was torn and tattered, and the foam seats were so badly deteriorated they exposed the rusted coil springs inside. On the floor was a small, pint-sized glass milk bottle from Sealtest dairy in Hackensack, NJ. Just above the rear-view mirror was a small safety pin and ribbon with a Saint Christopher medal hanging from the headliner.

Once again, my mind wandered to thoughts of those owners putting that medal there when the car was new, hoping that it would save them from any harm on the highways. Did they live to ripe old ages, or did the Saint Christopher medal fail to protect them from the harm that befell them? The junk yard took many twists and turns. Some cars were sprouting trees from their engine compartments and many of them were warmly covered in years and years of fallen dead leaves, befitting the rusted remnants that lay beneath.

One of my more frightening finds was an old 1960s ambulance. It looked like it just came off the streets of the fictional town of Mayberry from The Andy Griffith Show. It had two large, red pointy lights on the back that I imagined used to flash back and forth while speeding down the street toward a local hospital. The lights would be accompanied by a primitive wail from an old wind-up crank-style siren. It was painted half red and half white, and the side windows took up almost three quarters of its length. On one of the windows were the faded remains of a painted caduceus (the symbol of medicine). I felt a little apprehensive and was frightened to go into this one, but my fear gave way to curiosity. I opened one of the rusted side doors and cautiously stepped into the rig. The first thing I noticed were two or three stethoscopes hanging from a hook, their rubber tubing cracked and deteriorated, just barely attached to the ear tubes.

As I looked around, there were torn and ripped bed sheets and mattresses on gurneys, littered with deposits of mold and mildew. On one mattress, I saw the remains of what looked like human bones—a smattering of fragments of perhaps a jaw or a spine. I hoped that they were from a dead squirrel or raccoon that might have gotten in there and couldn't find its way out. Once again, my mind wandered to the final occupants of that last ride, the one that ended the journey of the once-valuable transport of a productive medical response team. I sat for a few more minutes, then spotted something odd next to one of the giant wheels on the gurney. I got up to get a better look. I picked up a limp and weathered teddy bear. It was missing an eye and one ear was almost completely torn off, exposing its waterlogged stuffing. I threw it back down and decided that I didn't want to think about that bear or to whom it belonged.

After a few more visits, I started collecting the metal auto emblems from different cars. I found the designs of the foreign cars particularly interesting, such as the red, white and blue flag emblem of the French-made Renault and the classy Mercedes star emblem. The Ford Mustang had a neat running horse combined with the red, white and blue banner background. The emblem of the Oldsmobile 88 was a sleek metal rocket ship, and some of the other companies spelled out the names in cursive metal writing, like the Maverick, Comet and Ford Fairlane. The Opal had its distinctive lightning bolt, and the Corvette had its famous crossed racing flags. I did collect enough emblems over the years to make a really nice wall hanging after cleaning and polishing each and every one of them. I don't know what happened to my work of art; it got lost in the shuffle after a few moves.

I spent many days going through that junk yard, enjoying the quiet and solitude; nothing but the sounds of birds and small mammals who made this sanctuary of broken and discarded metal their home. Those were the times I didn't think about death or destruction, only peace and contentment. There was still a lot of beauty to behold there; but in the end, it followed nature's creed: ashes to ashes, dust to dust… and rust to rust!

The Good Uncle

As kids, we learn a lot about our parents' families just by visiting them. I had lots of aunts and uncles, and from time to time we would have a Sunday visit with them. One of my uncles owned a hardware store in North Jersey. When we went to his home for dinner, my uncle would take some of us kids to the store to check up on the employees. I loved wandering down the halls of that store, exploring all kinds of mechanical and electrical gadgets. I would sometimes read about tools or other objects and know them by name; but I could never quite figure out what they looked like or how they worked. I learned what an auger, rasp and junction boxes were. Believe it or not, these trips to my uncle's store helped me build, create and repair many things over my lifetime.

One of my other uncles worked as a security guard for Palisades Amusement Park; and I often saw him in uniform, thinking that he was this big-time law officer protecting the public from the neighborhood crooks and thieves. What he really did was to make sure that kids didn't sneak onto rides without paying. One good perk for us was that he could get us lots of free tickets to go on rides at the park. On many summer nights, when we visited his family, he would take us all to the

park and get us in for free, then give us rolls of tickets to ride anything we wanted.

Uncle Frank had three daughters, and when the third one came around, he realized he needed to make more money; so he quit his job and invested all his savings into opening an IHOP restaurant. His first two years were not good. His employees stole from him. His expenses skyrocketed. He worked over 90 hours a week and it took a toll on his health and family. He managed to find good managers later on, and eventually opened a second and third restaurant. Once again, we kids got free dinners and desserts for as long as I could remember. It's funny, but I don't ever remember having meaningful conversations with any of my uncles. We would usually just say hello, and they would ask us about school; but there were never deeper connections made. Kids often make more meaningful relationships with the grandparents and cousins, but not so much with the aunts and uncles. I'm not sure why that is.

If you think about it, kids probably miss out on remarkably interesting and enlightening stories about their lives growing up, along with the struggles they had to make in a world so different than others'. Sure, they talked a lot about hard times, low wages, poor living conditions and keeping jobs; but kids today can't fully grasp those concepts because their lives have been made easier by all the modern conveniences and opportunities they have today. Perhaps the old saying that life was simpler and better in the olden days wasn't all that true.

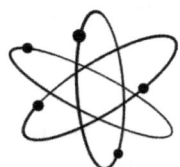

We Were All Broken Once

How many times did you blame your parents for the bad choices you made in your life? How many times did you fault your ninth-grade math teacher because you decided to be a car mechanic instead of being a statistician? Did your first crush on a person fail because you were too needy or demanding, or did you fail to make the right choice by training to be a barber instead of a management consultant? You can't blame your father for your grey hair if you got it by worrying about every little thing you screwed up in your life. You can't blame your third stage emphysema on your friend, Larry, who desperately tried to talk you out of smoking when you were a teenager. In a lot of ways, we're all broken, usually by the decisions we made or didn't make in life.

I was recently talking with a friend, and I mentioned that I wished my parents had taught me more about money and finances when I was growing up. I would probably be more successful in money management today if that were the case. He listened, then asked if my parents were rich or came from money. I said, "We were as poor as church mice!"

"Well, there you have it. If your parents didn't have two dimes to scrape together, they couldn't very well teach you about savings or investments now, could they?" We all are a product of not only our upbringing, but of our environment. If you lived in a fancy house and had all the things you ever wanted handed to you, you would never know humility or sacrifice. If you couldn't hold onto a job, you can't fault your parents or teachers because you were too lazy to learn the skills they were trying to teach you. Instead, you wound up broken. If you grew up in a low-income family and had to wear the same pair of tired old jeans three times a week, you thought twice about squandering your hard-earned dollars on milk shakes with your friends. So, your social life changes. You make the best of it because you are broken. The good thing about being broken is that you are not alone.

Everyone is at some point in their lives. We humans tend to seek out others who are broken, as well. It's like we are looking for someone to help us reassemble *our* broken pieces from *their* stash of broken pieces. If you are like me, you tend to seek out those who share the same status quo. Finally, the best thing about being broken is that you realize you're still human, and you can change anything about yourself and your life that you want. You don't need permission; you only need a reason and the drive. You can't fix everything at once, but you don't have to remain broken forever.

Cactus Gulch

I got my first Lionel train set when I was 10 years old. Although it was a Christmas present, I couldn't put it together until after the holidays. It wasn't because I didn't want to, mind you. There was just no room in the living room, dining room or even my bedroom, where I shared cramped quarters with my two messy brothers. I had to wait until my dad built me a table downstairs in the basement before I got the chance to play with my trains.

My first layout was primitive: a piece of used plyboard painted green with some circles and arcs cut out of it. I had to make do and cover them over with lichen and wood chips. The 3 by 5-foot board had nice sturdy legs, and I even had a small round stool to sit on next to the engineer's corner. I was overly excited.

I got out my old issues of *Model Railroader* and began to plot the towns I wanted to recreate. Many of the cities and towns the magazines described were much too big for me to model after, so I took bits and pieces of a few towns like Burlington, Vermont, Le Crosse, Michigan, and Chico, California. I figured that I could have a little fall and winter part of the northeast, tiny rural country farm landscape from the Midwest, and a desert and western town like they had on *Bonanza* and *Gunsmoke*. I spent hundreds of hours building and creating my towns. I didn't have a whole lot of money to spend on train stuff, so most of it I had to make myself. I got electrical wire and brown clay and fashioned my own trees. On the Vermont side, I even painted tiny bits of Play-Doh to look like apples for my apple trees.

On my country trees, I made them into stately oaks with acorns. Of course, some of them had to be on the ground because of the many squirrels on the farm. I made my own picket fences—white ones for the Vermont house to keep in the cows, and sturdy brown ones to corral all the horses on the ranch out west.

One of the houses in Chico had a nice backyard for the kids, including a pool. It took me three days to cut and fashion the in-ground pool out of balsa wood, paint and plastic sheets. It had a cute volleyball net across it and a bunch of colored noodles made from…

what else, painted spaghetti. I really got creative when I sliced off the head of a plastic figure and glued him on top of the water for a realistic looking water treader.

My snow for the mountains surrounding Burlington was created by using shaving cream mixed with baking soda. I added a little bit of fine sparkling confetti to make the snow glisten when I dimmed the street lighting. There was a homemade toboggan coming down the snowy hill, filled to the brim with neighborhood kids, and a small frozen pond where an old man sat with fishing pole in hand and a fish on the line. Of course, his trusty collie, Max, was sitting on the ice right next to him.

My western town took the most time of all. I had fashioned the town from my memories of Virginia City as seen on episodes of *Bonanza* in the '60s. Each of the 12 buildings that made up Cactus Gulch were hand-painted and weathered to look like they had been standing there for decades. A few of the saloon windows were cracked and made realistic by using crinkled up saran wrap, with every stretch mark outlined with a felt tipped marker.

My horses had plenty of troughs with dirty water in them, and there were plenty of stray cats and dogs chasing each other through the town streets. Luckily, I chose a time period where electricity was already in use, and it gave me a chance to use miniature lighting fixtures in each of the buildings on Main Street. Oh, and the bank was just being robbed, so the masked bandit and his cohort were attempting to mount their horses when they dropped their bags of loot; and the money was strewn around in the non-existent wind. I got really good at counterfeiting all those bills, considering they were the size of grains of rice.

When people came downstairs to the basement to see my masterpiece, one of the first things they noticed was the house of ill repute in Cactus Gulch. You see, I had to undress some of my plastic people and re-paint them to look slutty and loose. I had one woman hanging out of one of the upstairs windows with her buxom self quite exposed, and… well… she wasn't exactly selling candy to the children, that's for sure. I really enjoyed the many thousands of hours I spent down there building my miniature wonderland. We had to take it down once the kids got older to make another bedroom.

I'm not sure where the layout wound up, but I still have boxes and boxes of train stuff in the garage. I sold almost all the engines and cars a long time ago to get money to go to Hawaii. That trip was memorable, but not as much as my time spent building my very own miniature bit of America.

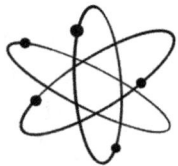

Ahh, Youth!

I don't have to tell most of you that once you are over 50, it's a bit more difficult to stay in shape and be healthy. The body says "Hey, lay off!" and you don't want to be a couch potato, so you ignore the negative thoughts and get your butt to the gym.

Wasn't life simpler when we were kids? As preteens you could go outside and run and jump, play kick the can, run around like crazy loons playing Hide and Seek, hit every piece of equipment at the playground, and even after three hours you were still raring to go. Nowadays, I do my one-hour workout with some crunches, leg lifts, pull downs, flys, and spend 15 minutes on the treadmill. Then I must call it quits. Where did we find all that energy when we were younger? We got by on five or six hours of sleep. We stayed up watching the *Late Late Show* and still made it through the rigors of high school the following day. I remember my senior year in school—going out with friends, eating crappy McFish things with overly salty fried foods, drinking the worst things, burning the candle at both ends and still managing to keep at least a "B" average. These days, if I don't get a decent nap at least twice a week, I'm worthless. Today, I give up that cold bottle of brew for a mix of low-fat cow juice mixed with almond liquid-something. It's supposed to be better for you. On top of that, I arrange my daily dosage of five assorted pills on my bathroom counter the night before, so I won't forget to take them the minute I wake up. I guess I'm lucky in that I only consume five instead of 15. I'm also blessed, as I am one of the few in my family who still has full use of their hips and knees. It's nice to think back to your youth, when life's cares were fewer, and stress was something for your parents to enjoy. Today, my happy hour is getting to bed around 9. Yeah, life is good.

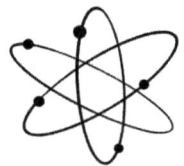

The Rheem Monster

I woke up to the sound of my own teeth chattering. After a few minutes of wondering why I could almost see my breath as I expelled air, I realized that once again the furnace had gone out. I sat up in bed and glanced at the bedroom window. Ice crystals had formed on the inner pane, only reinforcing the feeling that it was much colder than I realized. That old furnace had seen better days, even before we moved in some twenty-odd years ago, and it wasn't unusual for it to fail on some of the coldest winter mornings.

I hopped out of bed and shivered my way to the closet. I slipped on a pair of raggedy old slippers and threw on my trusty careworn terry robe. The old mercury thermometer from Miller's Meats registered a chilly 42 degrees, and that was INSIDE! I glanced back at the window and looked across the lawn at the more than two feet of freshly fallen snow from the night before. The morning sun starting peeking over the horizon and reflected a warm glistening off the surface of the snow. There had been no traffic on Mason Drive, and the plows hadn't been around yet.

There was a certain quietness to the neighborhood at this hour. No one was shoveling, no kids were playing, no howling winds left over from the night before.

The tiny, bare branches of the peach tree were laden with an inch or two of snow, and a couple of mourning swallows fought for the same branch where a single ray of sunshine illuminated it. As they landed, small tufts of snow fell to the ground and disturbed the silky unadorned surface below. Just for a moment, I forgot about my frostbitten nose and fingertips and remembered the more important task to get the furnace working again. I started down the creaky stairs to the basement, trying not to wake up anyone else in the house with my noise. The huge Rheem furnace lied dormant in the room like a sleeping giant dozing away. I peered through the small glassine window and, sure enough, the pilot light was out. Remembering the sequence took less than a minute, since I had done this so many times before. First, turn off the gas.

Take one of the very long wooden match sticks and light it. Slide the small, rounded pilot light cover to

the left and hold it there. Insert the lighted match all the way in, and hold it above the gas tube. Push the red button and hold it for 45 seconds. Next, turn the knob to the pilot lighting position and release the red button. If the light stays on, turn the gas valve back the other way. If the light still stays on, turn the knob to the ON position and wait for the monster to come to life. It did! I watched the three rows of heating elements turn blue as the gas started flowing, and after a minute or two, the main blower motor flew into action.

Once again, the thought of having to replace the old girl was averted and we were good again until who knew when. It took a good half hour for the house to get warm. I felt like a civilized human again, instead of a primitive Eskimo living in an Igloo.

Back in my room, I once again stared out the window, and by now our tiny town had awoken. The streets were trodden, driveways were starting to appear; and even a few adventurous kids were dragging sleds down the sidewalk, heading for the nearest hills to play. The icy frost on the inside of the window had melted away and left a small puddle of water on the sill. The sleeve on my robe soaked up most of it. The Miller's Meats thermometer was up to 60 degrees as I climbed back into my bed, ducking under the warm comforter for a short 15-minute Saturday morning nap.

Picnicking, Italian Style

Whoever heard of eating spaghetti and meatballs on a picnic? my friend Gene asked. I didn't answer him right away. Instead, I continued to load the mason jars of spaghetti sauce into the heavy cardboard box, then carried them out to the back of the pickup truck. The house was abuzz with activity as kids and adults trotted back and forth from the house and garage with camping supplies. Coleman stove: check! Large stock pot: check! Wooden spoons, colander, ladle and gas can: check! "Well, Gene, it's this way. We're Italians and we love our pasta. It's a whole lot easier to cook two or three pounds of spaghetti and heat up some sauce and meatballs than it is to cook 20 hamburgers, 15 hot dogs, 12 sausages, ribs, and all the stuff that goes along with that," I explained. My friend, Gene Soloway, was Jewish, and he came from a family of two. Our family numbered a dozen, give or take.

I loved packing up the truck when I knew we were going camping. Our usual place was Child's State Park near Dingmans Falls, Pennsylvania. If we were lucky, and most of the time we were, we got there early enough to snag one of the two covered pavilions near the creek. Each pavilion had four picnic tables in it, so it was plenty big for our family. Coolers were stacked on one table and the stove on another, along with piles of blankets, towels, flip flops, baseball bats, gloves and various other toys. Child's Park was the best place we knew to spend the day exploring the woods, take a dip in the icy cold water that flowed down the cliff, and enjoy a hearty plate of steaming spaghetti and meatballs with all the fixings, all out in nature's wonderland.

Once we arrived, a bunch of us kids would trek up the hill to the water pump with buckets and gallon jugs. Each of us would take turns pulling the handle of the pump up and down until the water started flowing. I would get the stove going. You had to fill a red container with unleaded gas and then pump a little nozzle up and down, filling it with air until you couldn't push it any longer. Then you opened the valve and lit a match. The gas started out yellow, and once it changed to blue you knew it was all set. The large

25-gallon stock pot would take a good hour to boil, but by then everyone was scattered all over playing and enjoying the outdoors. The grownups would throw the old bed sheets on the picnic tables and lay out the plastic dishes, enough for everyone in the group. We had loaves of Italian bread, dishes of creamy butter, bowls of tossed salad greens and plastic cups for the chilled red wine, which was cleverly disguised in chocolate milk containers. Once supper was about ready, we sent out a sentry to round up everyone.

One of my favorite things to do in the park was to rearrange the brook. After many months of rainstorms, there would be lots of downed branches in the way of the flowing water. My middle sister, Nora, and I liked to go up and down the rocks and remove the dead branches, free the piles of backed-up leaves and rearrange some of the rocks so the water could flow more easily. I'm not sure why, but doing that made us very happy.

After supper, we would all clean up the house, store all the gear and get the coffee pot and tea kettle going. There was almost always a couple of boxes of Italian pastries for dessert, along with the usual watermelon, cantaloupe and mixed fruit compote. After cleaning up, most of us would grab our walking sticks and start out on one of the many hiking trails that crisscrossed the park. If it was nearing the end of summer, the leaves would start to die off. In the fall, the intense afternoon sun would shine down through some of the trees, heating up the dense underbrush on the ground. I loved the smell of the leaves slightly baked from the bright sunlight. As we meandered through the trails, we would see squirrels or chipmunks gathering acorns and nuts and stashing them inside the hollows of the fallen trees. We would come across a single wooden bench lining the creek, where we could sit and take in the mesmerizing sound of the babbling brook. I also loved just sitting there for the longest time, especially if there were no other people around. I could really relax and let my mind wander. As the sun started to set, the kids would start drifting back to the pavilion, and everyone would indulge in coffee, tea, snacks and dessert. The trip home from the park was usually solemn, as most of the kids were just plum tuckered out and half asleep, and the adults just pretty much mellowed out from the day. You couldn't ask for a nicer day than spending it with good old-fashioned hearty Italian food, fun-loving families of energetic kids, cousins and the great outdoors. This made for the most perfect Italian picnic.

Father Fanelli's Magic Houdini Box

I never quite understood some of the concepts of the Roman Catholic religion. Sure, I went to a few Catholic schools and had to take catechism lessons like most of the kids in our Italian American neighborhood; but when you are a young kid of eight, some traditions just don't make any sense.

One of the stranger rituals was going to confession. On Saturdays, between 9:00 am and 11:00 am, kids were lined up to go see Father Fanelli in his special, magical Houdini box. When the Deacon called your name, you had to go inside this dark, damp closet where there was just enough light to see your hand in front of your face. I think they purposely let you sit there a few minutes to build up a little more fear and trepidation in you, like there wasn't enough already. You tried not to think of the verbal beating you were about to get by making shadow figures with your hands against the side wall. The light was so poor that my shadow rabbit looked oddly deranged, and my elephant's trunk looked more like a pink flamingo.

Suddenly, Father Fanelli would open the sliding wooden screen door and confront the next guilty kid. "Whenever you're ready, my son," he would say. "Bless me father, for I have sinned," I said back, sud-

denly trying to remember all of the bad things I did that might be considered sins. I whispered under my breath, *Should I tell him that I called my sister a wench? Should I mention that I borrowed $2 from my mother's purse with no intention of paying her back? Maybe I shouldn't bring up the fact that I accidentally cut open the toe on my brother's good school shoes as I was preparing to torture a cricket with my Boy Scout pen knife.* After a minute, I uttered to Father as softly as I could,

"I think I cursed twice and took the Lord's name in vain at least once."

"Anything else, my son?" I think the good Father knew I wasn't coming clean about a whole bunch of stuff, so I added one more minor incident to make it look plausible. "I think I also might have not honored my mother and father," I said. "In what way, my son?"

"Well, I might have been stubborn and rebellious once or twice."

"Do you regret your actions?" he inquired. "Yes, Father. I will try to be a better person from now on."

"Well then," he said, "For your penance you shall say one act of contrition, three Hail Marys, two Our Fathers; and you will pay back your mother the $2 you stole, give your brother your allowance for three weeks to buy new shoes, and you will compliment your older sister three times just for nothing."

"Yes, Father," I said, as I slithered off the wooden seat and opened the door to leave. I briefly turned back and asked, "How did you know?"

"The Lord works in mysterious ways, my son. Besides that, you need to learn how to whisper in a little lower voice."

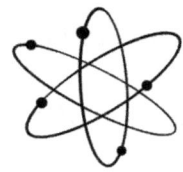

The Italian Evil Eye

On my eighteenth birthday, my mother sat me down in the kitchen and poured us each a small glass of Chianti. "Today, you are a man," she said. And so, in keeping with an age-old tradition in the Italian culture, she handed me a small gold foil box. I opened the box and took out the small square of white protective fiber. Underneath was a strange looking gold horn.

"What's this?" I asked. I wasn't ready for the story she began to tell, but I listened intently. "This is called a *corno*," she said, rolling the RRRRR's like a good dialect teacher. "When a boy becomes a man, he is presented with a *corno* by either his nonna or his mother," she went on. "It is not something you can buy for yourself; it must be given." At this point, my curiosity got the best of me, and I asked her what it meant. "It is meant to protect you against the evil eye, demons, and even Satan," she explained. "It will keep you safe."

My first thought was why she hadn't given it to me a year earlier when I really needed it. I had a terrible accident on my bike and ended up in Saint James hospital for two weeks with a few broken bones and a mild concussion. I didn't press the issue, so she continued on. "Some people call it a *cornicello*, which means a small horn in Italian. The amulet was adapted from both Greek and Roman mythologies dating back from the fifth century BC, and it's said to promote fertility, virility and good luck."

I picked up the tiny twisted golden horn and held it up to the light. "Where did you get it, mom?" I asked. "Well, it came from a small souvenir shop down in Little Italy; and I didn't pay full price for it, either" she said. Once again, I was curious and asked her what she meant by that. Did she bargain with the sales clerk or did she have a discount coupon?

"Oh, no," she explained. "According to tradition, one cannot pay full price for a *corno*, and it must not be bought for yourself, or the wearer will have nothing but bad luck." I sipped on the Chianti and listened to the explanation. "It was $20, but I asked the salesman to give me back a penny. He knew exactly what I meant and handed me back a shiny 1967 penny."

About a week later, I went into Prager's Jewelers and bought myself a beautiful 18-carat gold rope chain and put my *corno* on it. Soon after, I noticed that I was beginning to get darker facial hair, and the very faint moustache that I had since I was seven years old had finally started to show. I remembered Mom mentioning the word, "virility". Hmmm, I thought. Was this really a magical link from adolescence to manhood, or was it just my normal hormones kicking in? I didn't question it, but I am very superstitious about my horn, and I have been wearing it every day since then—well… except for a few times when I removed it to have an MRI or a CAT scan done on my bruised body parts.

The Little Fraudsters

My little sister wandered into my bedroom and saw me sitting at my desk, writing. "What are you doing?" she asked. "I'm writing a letter to the Lionel company," I said. "What for?" she asked. "Well, I just bought a couple of brand-new cars for my train set, and the couplers keep falling off."

"What are couplers?" she asked. I picked up the closest boxcar with the painted Lifesavers candy roll on it and showed her the part of the car that makes it hook onto the one in front of it on the track. "See? It just fell off," I said as I pointed to the malfunctioning coupler. "They should be made better than that," I said. "Lionel used to make such good quality trains. Now, they're getting made cheaper and cheaper. Even the wheels seem flimsy. I'm writing to ask them for a replacement car," I said. "Will they just send you a new one?" she asked. "I hope so," I replied.

About a week later, the postman delivered a package. The return address was *The Lionel Corporation of Hillside, New Jersey*. I tore into the package; and there, inside, was a nice letter of apology and... not one, but three brand new box cars. I was so excited, I started yelling "I hit the jackpot, I hit the jackpot!" My sister, who was close by, came running into my room and saw my excitement. "See, I told you it was a good thing to write to them!"

A few days later, I found my sister, Maryann, writing a letter to the Mars company. When I asked her why she was writing to the candy company, she explained that the chocolate on these particular Mounds bars was not that good. "I bought this from the candy machine at school; and when I opened the package, the chocolate coating was all whitish." She showed me the affected chocolate candy, and I had to agree. It didn't look all that appetizing, and nothing at all like the mouthwatering photo shown on the wrapper.

About a week later, a package arrived for my sister from the M&M Mars company in Hackensack, NJ.

Inside was a nice letter of apology and a whole box of 24 brand new Mounds bars. You can imagine the expression on her face at the windfall she just acquired. A few days later, another surprise parcel arrived. This one was from the Lady Clairol company. It seems that the package of 18-count pink Doozy Doo curlers was missing one. Not one to be cheated out of a single curler, a nicely worded letter was written to the consumer complaint department by my other sister, Judy. This time she was rewarded by not only a supply of pink and turquoise curlers, but also a 9-ounce bottle of premium setting gel.

I think I might have unleashed a greedy demon in my sisters that I had never seen before, because now they started finding all kinds of faults with all kinds of products. They began a crusade of letter writing, citing defects, imperfections and flaws in everything from pantyhose to breakfast cereal.

Day after day, the postman would deliver small and medium boxes, manila envelopes, mailing tubes with all kinds of replacement items with lots and lots of letters of apology from dozens of companies. Some companies would even send them replacement coupons good for free stuff just for letting them know about the many quality control issues that were occurring on the production lines of the various factories.

This went on for at least a year or two, and they finally wore themselves out trying to remember which companies they had defrauded and which ones they hadn't. So, rather than get called out for criminal deceptions for personal gain, they decided to give up the letter writing campaigns. It's probably a good thing, too, because a lot of products that were made in foreign countries turned out to be pretty crappy. My sisters would be writing letters until their fingers fell off.

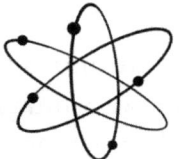

S&H Green Stamps

Saturday mornings around our house were kind of hectic, as one can well imagine. With that many kids running around, breakfast was total chaos. The frying pan was filled with scrambled eggs, the coffee pot was percolating, and the old two-slice toaster didn't stop until the entire loaf of Wonder Bread was used up. Kid after kid would come down for breakfast, grab a plate, dish out some eggs and oatmeal, toast and orange juice, and scarf it all down within minutes, barely stopping to breathe between bites. If one of us was late for breakfast, it might mean last night's cold pasta *fagioli*.

I managed to get in on the second shift and dished myself out the last scrapings of the scrambled eggs. I grabbed the last two pieces of bread from the Wonder Bread bag and snickered, "How come nobody eats the ends?" I hated the end pieces, too; but if that's all there was, I couldn't complain too much. I popped them into the toaster and sat there patiently waiting… and waiting. Finally, I realized those tiny little wires weren't lighting up red like they should. I shook the toaster, pushed the lever up and down a few times, but still nothing. Darn!

"Mom," I yelled, "Someone broke the toaster!"

Mom chimed back, "Well, there isn't much I can do about that now. I have to get the laundry started or you kids will be wearing last week's underwear all over again."

After the morning rush was over, I decided to tinker with the toaster. I discovered that one of the tiny heating wires was broken, so this toaster had just seen its last slice of bread.

I pulled out the Sears catalog and flipped through the pages of small appliances. I searched for the toasters and found one that sold for $12. "If we all pooled our money together, we could get a new one from Sears," I said. Mom replied, "I have a better idea. Go grab as many kids as you can find and gather around the dining room table."

"Okay," I said, and rushed off into the back yard. I rounded up my two brothers and four sisters and we all marched into the dining room and sat down. Mom came in with a huge plastic cookie tin and plopped it on the table. She started pulling out stamps—S&H green stamps, plaid stamps, blue stamps and gold stamps. Then she gave each one of us a book. "Everyone take a book and start licking," she demanded. "I'm sure we have enough stamps to get two toasters."

Back in the late fifties and throughout the sixties, every grocery store, gas station—and even some department stores—gave out free stamps when you purchased food and gas. Mom saved every single stamp she could get her hands on. She even traded with some neighbors' green ones for plaid ones, since the green ones were worth more.

For the next hour or so, we licked and licked and pasted and pasted. We eventually filled up thirteen green stamp books, eight plaid stamp books and three blue stamp books.

Later that week, we took a ride to the Green Stamp Redemption Center, where we picked out a beautiful, brand new, *four*-slice toaster. And it only cost us eleven filled books of stamps. Breakfast at our house was finally modernized.

Nail Clipper Nuisance

I must have been only about eight or nine years old the first time Dad cornered me and handed me a pair of shiny new nail clippers. "Clip my toenails, Junior," he said. So, he sat me down and showed me how to use this funny looking snipping device. "First, you pull up on this little lever and then turn it around and it will stick up," he explained. "Then, put the nail between the two sharp blades and push the lever." I can do that, I thought to myself. He took off his sock, sat back on the brown leather easy chair and put his foot up on the matching ottoman. I stared at his big toe. The nail was all brittle and yellowed and frankly not very appealing to look at. I was having second thoughts, but I realized that Dad had just come from the doctor's office and found out he had a serious heart issue. I didn't want to upset him more, so I inched closer to the large yellow toe and held the clippers around the center of his nail. As I pushed down, the metal claws chomped down and spit off a good chunk of the nail. It went flying. "Don't worry about them; we'll get them later," he said. I wasn't the least bit worried about flying bits of nails, but rather the sound of the clipper. It made my teeth cringe. For whatever reason, I detested the noise. The loud, distinct SNIP echoed through my brain every time the tool bit down on another toenail. Dad didn't notice my discomfort, just my lack of enthusiasm as I went from one digit to another. SNIP, SNIP, SNIP. The more it snipped, the more irritated I became. Finally, after going through all ten toes, I put his socks back on. He put his hand out and I handed him the clippers. He patted me on the head and walked away. I grabbed the amber ashtray from the cigarette stand near the chair and began searching for all the yellow toenail fragments.

To this day, I won't use a genuine nail clipper, as it still gives me the creeps. I prefer to use a nice sharp pair of paper scissors. They're so much quieter, and they get the job done just as well.

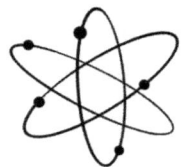

The Famous Mr. F's Paddle

There is something special to be said about teachers. We could all probably say we had at least one favorite teacher growing up who left a distinct impression on us in some form or another. I've had a few.

In my freshman year at Raritan Township High, my general science teacher, Mr. Federovich, left such a mark. Like many other teachers in the 1960s, he held two jobs. Mr. F. was a pretty big guy, towering over 6'4" and weighing in about 240 lbs. This was the perfect size for a man who coached football. He was intimidating to most of the kids, and his deep boisterous voice only proved that he was not one to take any kind of bull from his puny teen minions.

My first couple of days in Mr. F.'s General Science class were quite interesting. He made each of his students stand up in front of the class and introduce themselves to everyone. I, being kind of shy, was glad to have a last name starting with "R", since he went down the list alphabetically. When it was my turn, I slowly inched off my seat, and with my head down, proceeded to the front of the classroom. After announcing my name, Mr. F. asked if I had any particular skills, other than athletic, that I wanted to share with the class. My mind wandered for a few moments, and I realized I had none. Other kids mentioned their ability to draw or paint, and some amazed the class with their musical talents for the piano or trumpet. One 15-year-old regaled the class with his proficiency at mastering the Rubik's Cube in 65 seconds. As I thought harder, I knew I had to come up with something, so I lied. "I help my father build furniture… tables, desks and chairs," I said. I heard a couple of kids blurt out some oohs and ahhs, then waited for him to say something. "See me after class, Mr. R.," he said. I immediately started to sweat. What did I do to deserve a special audience with my science teacher? Once class let out, I lagged behind. Mr. F. came up to me and handed me a sheet of notebook paper. I stared at it for a second. Sketched on the paper was an outline of a football player all dressed in his uniform, helmet and all. He looked like he was running, arms tucked in by his sides and his right back leg lunging forward. With an inquisitive look on my face, I started to ask him about the sketch. Before I could get out a word, he asked me if I could make this out of wood. Once again, with a puzzled look, I asked him what he meant.

He explained, "As you probably know, I'm the head football coach here at Raritan." He went on. "I'm very good as a coach, but I do lack certain people skills; and discipline is not one of my strong points. I need something to show these young whippersnappers that I mean business. This is going to be my football paddle. I want this made out of ¾" plyboard, and I want the feet to be the handle. I want it painted with our school colors and I want the face of this running back to be mean and frightening."

"Do you mean you want to use this to give whacks to those big, huge guys if they do something wrong?" I questioned. "Yep," he said. "When I get through with them, they are going to know who is boss around here; and if they get the slightest bit out of hand, they will get whacked by Mr. F.'s paddle right on their tender behinds."

For some strange reason, this brought a great big smile to my face. Knowing that in some small way, I would be an accomplice to Mr. Federovich's school of dumb jocks discipline made me quite happy.

I took the sketch home. The following day, I brought it, along with an 18" by 24" piece of plyboard, to Mrs. Gibson in the art department. Since I couldn't draw a stick figure to save my life, I asked if she had a student who could draw the football guy onto the plyboard. I explained what I was doing and before I knew it, a couple of sophomores were designing a menacing looking football jock onto the board.

It took another few days, and with the help of my woodshop teacher, Mr. Puhlfurst, and a trusty 27" bandsaw in the shop, our mean and green Mr. F's paddle was ready for painting. You should have seen the look on Mr. Federovich's face when I unveiled the finished project. It was like the mad scientist when he first discovered that his Frankenstein monster was alive.

It wasn't long before I got to see my creation in action, for not only was it used to keep the jocks in line, but it came in handy for another of Mr. F's pet peeves. You see, if you were supposed to be in his 9:20 am General Science class, you had better be in your seat exactly at 9:20, because at 9:21 he shut and locked the door. If you should happen to be late, he would open the door and escort you to the front of his class, bend you over his big wide desk and you would then be introduced to the business end of the now-famous Mr. F's paddle.

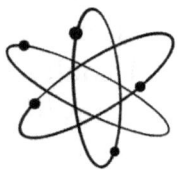

Ah, Ya Mother Wears Combat Boots

When the bullies at my high school couldn't think of anything to say to you to make you cringe with fear, they reverted to this: "Ah, ya mother wears combat boots." I never quite understood what that meant, but I knew it was bad.

My mother didn't own a pair of combat boots, even though she commanded a group of the most disruptive, ungrateful and thoughtless kids ever: her children. She managed to keep us all in line with just a sensible pair of flat loafers, which brought me back to the question of why the bullies insisted that Mom's wearing of Army footwear was such a terrible thing. I asked a professor of linguistics at school if he could clarify this for me, and his explanation was as follows.

"It's a catch phrase, sort of like 'ya fadder's moustache' or other variations, like 'ya mutter drives a tank' or 'Ya mutter wears cotton drawers.'" He went on, "Of course, in order for any of these sayings to have substance, they must be said with a heavy Brooklyn accent, or the meaning is completely lost."

Okay, that explains a little; but I wasn't convinced that my bully nemesis was saying that to make me appreciate his affection for vulgar east coast euphemisms. I was determined to find out more.

I advanced my fact-finding mission and went straight to the head English professor. His first answer was neither enlightening nor believable. "You see, young man… after World War II, Army surplus stores sold a lot of used military stuff. A person could go in and purchase a pair of inexpensive, but long-lasting, army boots for only a few bucks. Young ladies snapped them up faster than young men."

I wasn't convinced by that answer, so I prodded him for alternatives. "Well, I didn't want to go this far, but since you asked… the consensus was that this saying meant that your mother was a prostitute."

"Whoa!" I said, "Who are you calling a prostitute?"

"Here is the explanation," he went on. "It is said that during World War II, a number of staff sergeants would supply their troops with desirable women companions to keep up their morale. Some of these fine ladies would be seen sneaking out of the men's tents half naked and wearing a GI's Tee-shirt or fatigues. Some of them even borrowed the soldiers' boots to keep as souvenirs. The guys, in turn, would keep a number of the ladies' undergarments as a memento of the evening."

Well, now that I had a complete understanding of the statement, I was fully armed with a jaw-dropping retort. I was sure that even the smartest of these bully dimwits didn't have a clue as to what that statement meant. So, from that point on, when confronted by a bully slur, in my best Brooklyn accent I just said, "Ahh, ya fadder slept wit who-ers!" That shut them up!

My Fully Human Self

I once belonged to a group of college students who regularly went on outings together to discover themselves and their world. They were a mix of straight, gay, black, Asian, white and other races. Sometimes our treks would include about seven to ten people, sometimes more. I signed up for a weekend retreat through the student union at the University of South Florida, interestingly called "Insight through Shamanism."

At the time, I had no idea what a shaman was, so I did a little research. The shaman was a person, usually of Native American descent or other indigenous tribes, who was said to possess the ability to achieve visionary states of consciousness. A shaman could redirect a focused awareness away from everyday physical reality and into a hidden, inner world while still remaining awake—a sort of enhanced meditation.

The more I read, the more I was intrigued. So, I asked myself what a person would gain from such an experience, but I came up empty.

I asked a good friend of mine, Michael Rennie, to give me some insight, and he did. "Think of it as a way to restore power to yourself if you feel that you are being drained of that power by something you can't control," he said. Restore power, I thought to myself.

I can relate to that, being in the field of electronics. I asked Michael if he was going on this field trip, and he said he signed up for it. "Oh, great," I said. "We can do it together and I won't feel so afraid."

"You will have to do a little soul searching before we go so that you have a solid reason to do this," he said. "Just ask yourself what you want to get rid of in your life that's holding you back from being your fully human self. Is it something someone did to you physically? Is there something in your past that keeps you from achieving your goals?"

Wow! This was getting a bit heavy, I thought. "I'll have to give this some serious thought," I said. About two weeks went by, and the trip was coming up for the following Friday night.

A bus arrived on campus with the destination, ANYWHERE, in the upper window. "I guess that's us," I said to Michael as we climbed aboard. Our welcome packet that had arrived a week earlier told us what to pack and a few things to expect; but it never prepared me for what was about to happen.

The bus drove for about two hours through a pretty desolate and remote part of northern Florida, and we finally arrived at what looked like an old campground. There, scattered among the old log buildings, were a few tepees, a couple of herb gardens and a couple of paths that led in different directions. We were escorted to the largest building, went in, and were told to drop our gear over beside a wall. "Take a seat, people," we were instructed. "In front of you, you'll find a piece of burlap, a black crayon, some string, tobacco and a pinch of corn meal. Most of us had no idea what was going on. Were we going to do some arts and crafts? Was this some kind of skill test to see if we had a decent amount of manual dexterity? It soon all came together.

The leader, a man called Homer, started barking out instructions. "Take the piece of burlap and the crayon and start writing. I want you to write down three reasons you are here. Is there someone out there who hurt you? Is there an obstacle in your life that you are unable to climb? Is there a person you love who doesn't love you back? Did you do something wrong that you want to atone for?" The questions kept coming. Homer started walking around the room, staring people directly in the face and barraging them with questions, like he was interrogating us for the Inquisition.

It echoed through my little brain time and time again. At the tender young age of 10, I could hear my father's words, *That boy is a sissy!* My mother would, of course, defend me by saying something like, "No, he's just a little shy and quiet."

I suppose I always hated my father for teasing me like that, but I also suspected him of being just like me when he was a kid. You see, I was the sensitive one, the curious one, the one with the brains. I hated the things he and my brothers loved. Cars, sports and fishing were just not for me.

My father died at a young 44 years of age, and I never really got the chance to tell him how much I loved him, despite the emotional rollercoaster he put me through.

I reached for the black crayon and the burlap. I started to think of what to write. I wanted to get rid of the hatred I had for my father. I wanted to get rid of the pain and the relentless anger I felt every time I relived those memories of ridicule and mockery that I received from him. I thought to myself, "Could this ritual finally bring me some internal peace?"

I wrote down my intentions. We were instructed to put a little tobacco and corn meal into the center of the burlap, then tie up the pouch with string. We were to carry this around with us throughout the entire weekend until it was called for in one of the ceremonies.

After settling in, preparing our bunks and storing our trivial belongings, we started sharing our lives with the others. We sat outside on straw bales in a circle. A fire was kept lit throughout the entire weekend somewhere in the compound. It was a tradition to have a fire going while the spirits were in the camp.

I participated in a lot of different rituals that weekend, but the one I remember the most really helped me immensely in dealing with my abusive father.

All 16 of the men were sitting together in a circle on the straw bales. Homer entered the circle and split us up into two groups. The odd-numbered men were going to play the part of the fathers, and the even-numbered ones were to be the sons. I was number eight.

The fathers got up and started marching around the outer circle to a drumbeat. After about five minutes, they stopped. Each placed his right hand on the shoulder of the man in front of them. One by one, the fathers turned to the sons and asked them what it was that they always wanted to say to their father but never did. I watched intently as one by one the sons were confronted. Finally, I felt a hand on my shoulder and turned around, expecting to see this stranger named Dave. Instead, I saw my own father standing there. His brown curly hair was messed up as it always was, and his hazel green eyes starred at me with profound meditation. He had that stern look on his face, and I sensed immediate aggression. I stood motionless and placid. I kept looking at this stocky man waiting for him to yell, or something. I relived this fear in my mind a million times when I was confronted by my father's turbulent temper. I took a deep breath and opened my mouth.

The figure took his index finger and placed it over my lips, and what I heard from this man was totally unexpected. He told me how much he missed me and how important I was to him in his life. He told me he was wrong for belittling me and that he had the greatest respect for my own personal beliefs. Then, this man… this exhilarant man, reached out and put both his arms around me, hugged me and told me he loved me. There are no words I could write here to describe that moment. My thoughts were fervid, and I was filled with intense emotion. I stared once again into his eyes and saw my father fade away.

That experience helped me to finally reconcile most of the issues I had carried all those years about my relationship with my father. But there was one more ritual I shared on that fateful weekend that cemented it all together.

It was early Sunday morning around 4:00 when we

were awakened by the distant sound of drumming in the camp. The sounds grew stronger as my tent mates and I wearily rose from our cots. Just then, a messenger from the tribe stuck his head in the doorway. Even though it was dark, we could see that his face was painted with bright colors, and he was wearing a headdress of some sort. We were told to put on some clothes and shoes, not to talk, and follow him.

We quickly dressed and followed him out into the perimeter of the camp. It was still quite dark, and there was an eerie smell in the air. A thin layer of mist hovered above the clay earth and moved ever so slightly as we shuffled our feet along. Once my eyes adjusted to the darkness, a feeling of both excitement and nervousness came over me. Little by little, all the men from the cabins had gathered together in the clearing. The messenger raised a staff adorned with feathers and ribbons, then motioned us to follow him into the forest.

Although we had walked through these woods numerous times throughout the weekend, this path seemed unfamiliar to me. Aside from the sounds of hard soles hitting the ground and a few morning sparrows, no noises were uttered. After a few more minutes, we came into another clearing. There, in front of us, stood four large canvas teepees. We were divided up among them and told to sit on the cold, damp floor until we were called.

When we had first arrived in camp, we were all given Indian names. Now, I anxiously awaited hearing my Moon-dog name being called. About fifteen minutes went by, and one by one, the others in my group were called out. I was almost the last one when my name was finally called. I was instructed to go into the next teepee. As I entered, a warrior took hold of my arm and forcefully sat me down in front of the chief. He lifted my head up and began taking paint brushes from his three assistants. With each different color, he made strokes across my face and chanted. After about seven strokes, he lifted me from the stool and gestured at me to join the other painted men.

By this time, the hidden moon had peeked out from behind the clouds, and I got my first glimpse of my war-painted buddies. The bold streaks of red, yellow, green and blue across our faces glowed in the faint moonlight, almost iridescent. We weren't allowed to talk, so I just grinned, wondering if I looked as strange as they did.

As soon as the last man was painted, the warrior motioned for all of us to follow him. Once again, we started back into the forest. After a short while we came across yet another clearing. A large bonfire was burning in the middle. Ropes were arranged around the fire, and at the far edge there stood a large pole. It was adorned with feathers, animal skins and large lengths of beads hanging from the top to the ground.

When we reached the outer perimeter, the drumming sounded again. Each of us was given a drum, bongo or rattle. We were told to enter the circle and make as much noise as we could with the instrument we were given. Around we went. After five or six revolutions, I felt a sense of serenity and completeness. My mind went blank, and I was consumed in the rhythmic beat of the pounding sounds of drums and bongos. It's funny how a simple beat can make you feel so relaxed and calm. Suddenly, I caught sight of another warrior jumping out of the woods. He ran over to the man in front of me, grabbed him, and told him to enter the ring of fire and drum. He was told to pray to the spirits to let him pass. The rest of the men were summoned in the same manner, and eventually we were all in the center surrounded by fire, drumming and chanting.

One by one, we were touched on the forehead and asked if we were ready. The man to my right reached into his pocket and removed the little burlap sack containing his wishes and threw it into the fire. A large puff of white smoke appeared and seemed to linger there for a few seconds; then, as suddenly as it came, it faded away.

I was next. I stopped drumming and turned to face the inferno before me. I reached into my pocket and withdrew my burlap pouch. I dangled it in front of my face trying to recall exactly what I had written. A few seconds passed, then I flung it into the raging fire.

The pouch ignited and released a huge puff of white smoke. It rose up above the flames and transformed itself into a letter "L" as if to mimic my father's Italian given name, Lunardo. Seconds later it was gone. I took a deep breath of the cold crisp morning air and exhaled it slowly, methodically thinking of what I just witnessed.

In that instant, I knew what it all meant. I had thrown the fear of my father into that flame. In that

instant, I had let go of the intense hatred for the man who had reveled in putting me down. I was always labeled Junior because in his eyes, I was less than a man, a weak and feeble excuse for his perfect oldest son. In my moment of emancipation, I wiped away that title of Junior and finally became the man *I* wanted to be.

A few moments later, the warrior confronted me once again. "Are you ready now?" he asked. "Yes," I replied, nodding my head. I proceeded past the tall post and gathered with all the others. One by one, I was hugged by all those who had gone before me. My eyes were filled with tears, and I felt so exhilarated. I never in all my life felt so accepted, so loved, so needed. The warrior came and stood in front of me. He handed me the talking stick and asked me to share my thoughts with the group.

I took a big, deep breath and spoke. "For many years, I never felt truly whole. Parts of me were broken. Goals I wanted to reach were never achieved because I always felt I was never good enough. I let others crush my dreams before they were ever realized. But tonight, I defeated my demons and broke free from the bonds of oppression that held me captive for years. Tonight, I can honestly say, I have become my most fully human self."

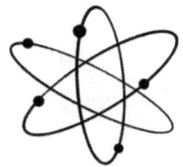

The Sound of Symphony Music

I was sad to hear that Andy, my newly engaged brother-in-law-to-be, was heading off to Vietnam. My sister and her boyfriend had been dating a little more than a year when he was called to serve. However, I wasn't sad to find out that he could get electronic equipment through the Army PX at ridiculously low prices. I put in a request for a brand-new pair of English-made stereo speakers from Wharfedale. These were amazing huge floor speakers that made your stereo sound like Lincoln Center Symphony Hall in New York City. The day they were delivered, I was in my glory.

In the house I grew up, we had a wall that divided the sections of the house, but the wall was only three quarters high. In the kitchen was a doorway that led to the basement. In the living room, my dad had broken out the inner wall above the stairs and built a much-needed closet. After most of my older sisters moved out, I turned it into a stereo closet.

I purchased a really nice stereo receiver from the Heath company. They sold electronics in kit form that enabled consumers to build items themselves. I loved building things, so this was right up my alley. The instruction manual was like reading *War and Peace*, with many pages of parts, blow-up diagrams

and schematics. It was very well done, and the company assured you that if you followed the directions to the letter, you could not fail. The stereo contained about eight printed circuit boards with hundreds of electrical components like resistors, capacitors and transistors. It took me about a month to complete, but it worked like a charm and the sound was remarkable. I positioned the two Wharfedale speakers on the top of the wall partition on either end, and the living room became a vibrant concert hall.

I had a collection of vinyl records on the Command label that were mostly percussion style. Most of the recordings started out by having just the left speaker channel, then it would drift over to the right speaker. Almost every tune had a variety of instruments that would fade between the two speakers, and you could truly hear the stereo separation with remarkable distinction. Over the next few years, Andy managed to get me a really good quality record changer, reel-to-reel tape recorder, and even a portable car stereo.

The days of elaborate stereo systems are long gone. The once popular stacks of separate tuners, amps, equalizers, pre-amps, turntables and reverbs are few and far between; but lately, there seems to be a renewed interest in old vinyl records and turntables. Today's generation of adults is finding out that the quality of those olden-day electronic marvels can't compare to the sound quality of the inferior tiny iPod headphones or the raspy and tinny Bluetooth speakers. Even with the tiny scratches in the records and the pops and skips, the quality of those old discs was absolutely amazing.

I guess, just like the clothing industry, if you hold onto a pair of elephant bell bottoms from the 1970s long enough, they might once again become popular. God, I hope not.

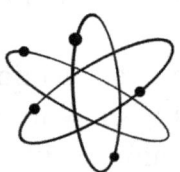

I'm Not So Red-Blooded as I Thought

I came out in October of 1983. I was 35 years old at the time, and had known almost all my life that I was gay. You've probably heard stories of kids who knew they weren't quite like all the others growing up. I was one of those kids. I liked to read, and I wasn't interested in cars or sports. So, I knew I was a little different—a socially incorrect boy in the Atomic Age. In my younger years, I also tended to notice more men than women, but I didn't think much about it at the time. However, once I hit puberty, the other boys my age began noticing and talking about girls a lot. They even started to talk about having crushes on girls. That's when I started to realize I might be more different than I thought—*atomically incorrect*. That's because I also began to have my own share of crushes; but my crushes were on male movie stars, sports figures and teachers.

One of my earliest recollections was watching the *Ozzie and Harriett* TV show in the 1960s. Ricky Nelson caught my eye, along with thousands of mostly teen-aged girls at the time. Like a lot of other celebrities, he did personal appearances at malls and movie theaters, and the press was always there to record the events. I remember watching the TV news and seeing all those teenage girls swooning over Ricky as he belted out his popular tunes, like *Hello Mary Lou* or *Travelin' Man*. I remember thinking that there must have been at least a few guys in those audiences who had the same thoughts as I did. In my mind, they were probably hiding their feelings and pretending to be good loyal boyfriends to some of the girls. They probably tagged along to make fun of the girls' idols or to make sure that their girlfriends didn't get friendly with those famous performers.

But, what if some of those guys were actually there because, like me, they were secretly attracted to guys like Ricky Nelson? You gotta admit, he was really cute with his dreamy, blue deep-set eyes and dark black wavy hair… not to mention his sexy deep voice.

If things were different then, I would have had a life-sized poster of him hanging in my bedroom instead of a phony poster of Raquel Welch or Ann Margaret. I probably could have gotten away with a poster of Joe Namath or Clint Eastwood, because these guys were perceived to be both male and female idols and those rough and tumble guys were admired by both sexes. The notion that every red-blooded American boy wanted a poster that combined his favorite two things—fast cars and sexy girls—was beginning to change. I certainly didn't want a huge picture of some sexy, bikini-clad beach blonde hanging on my wall, and I wasn't the least bit interested in photos of a fancy, overpriced, apple-red 4-speed muscle car hanging there, either.

Attitudes about sexuality were just beginning to

evolve in the early '60s. With the Vietnam war ever present and in the whole anti-establishment culture, men like me were beginning to experiment with their sexuality in ways never before tried. Men weren't afraid to wear loud, multi-colored, somewhat feminine designed clothes in an effort to blend in with their swinging generation of peers. Luckily for me, I didn't. I preferred the clean-cut, boy next door look and clothing. Maybe that's why I was attracted to guys like Ricky Nelson, Bobby Vee and Gene Pitney.

A lot of teens like myself kept in the know about their favorite celebs by buying magazines, like *Tiger Beat* and *Rona Barrett's Hollywood*. Not only could I get the latest gossip, but they supplied me with some of the hottest male pin-ups printed. There was even a short period where hairy-chested men were all the rage, and I developed an appreciation, putting it mildly, for those types of guys.

It would be many years later that I finally accepted my sexuality as being normal and not an affliction, as the medical field labeled it back then. I grew up meeting many wonderful guys, enjoying intimacy with some, sharing common tastes with others, and learning what it was like to be who I was meant to be… just me, who happens to be gay.

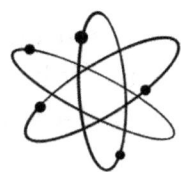

My Cat, Max: My Best Friend

Max passed away June 21, 2019. He lived an exceptionally long life for a cat, but there wasn't a day that went by when he wasn't loved or didn't love back.

I acquired him from a friend who was moving into a home with two large dogs, so it wasn't a good fit for Max. This was way back in 2003. Max had to first adapt to living with two other cats whom he would eventually accept as his brother and sister, but that took some time. He finally came around.

Max was short for Maximillian—kind of a strange name for a half tabby, half Siamese feline; but since he was already used to it, I kept it. He had the most beautiful turquoise blue eyes that sparkled like opals in the sunlight. His fur was tiger-striped with browns, greys and some black lines. The tip of his nose was pure pink.

I never knew his birthplace, but I think it was somewhere in Des Moines, Iowa. Although he was born in the Midwest, he seemed to exhibit the qualities of a cat born in a big city. He was as curious a cat as you would expect, and never missed an opportunity to get in trouble by letting his curiosity get the best of him.

I once found him nestled in the dryer among my freshly dried clothes after I left its door open to grab a phone call. He peeked his little head out between a

pair of white boxers and a dish towel and gave me a little whimper as if to say, "Don't remove me just yet. It's so toasty in here." Unlike most common cats, Max's Siamese heritage gave him back feet similar to a rabbit's. They were quite long and tapered, which gave him the ability to jump much higher than his siblings. So, it wasn't uncommon for me to find him at times perched up on the tallest bookshelf or the top of the refrigerator.

Unfortunately, his jumping landed him in the vet hospital with a broken left foot. There was a half-wall partition above the staircase, and one day, he miscalculated its width while jumping up and went completely over and landed on the third step below. Luckily, I was there and saw it happen. Broken leg and all, he tried to walk back up the stairs while in a daze and was meowing painfully the whole time. I rushed him over to the vet and they took X-rays. He had a single fracture of his hind leg bone.

For the next three weeks, you could hear him coming and going, his plastered leg clunking along the wooden floors sounding like a peg-legged pirate on the bow of a ship. He spent a good deal of that time in his own little cage with his own water, food bowl and a small litter box conveniently located nearby to cut down on his commute. My good friend, Maggie, stopped by every afternoon while I was at work to check on him and make sure he was comfy.

Cats love to cuddle, but they do so on their terms. Max was no exception. Since I slept with my bedroom door closed, he would frequently scratch on the door and meow loudly enough to drown out the sound of my small fan. Being a light sleeper, I would crawl out of bed and open the door to let him in. Immediately, he would jump up on the bed and get close to my face. I would lift the covers just enough to let him crawl in. He would go all the way down to my legs, turn around, then come back up and lay close to me with his head on my arm. This was almost a daily routine for him, especially on weekends when I would get to sleep in a little bit.

After a half hour or so, he would get a bit too warm, crawl out and sleep on the comforter at my feet. Once

I finally got out of bed, I would go into the bathroom and sit on the throne. Max would come in and lay his head right down next to my left foot and nudge it a bit. I knew he wanted me to rub his cheeks with my big toe. He absolutely loved when I did that. As soon as I stopped, he would nudge my foot again for me to keep doing it. I kept my toenail long on that toe just to please him in the mornings.

One of Max's favorite foods was tortilla chips. Strange, I know; but he knew the sound of that bag opening and came running from wherever he was to get some. He loved the white restaurant strips best. He also liked just a tiny bit of milk occasionally, so I spoiled him with it at times. Like his brother and sister, he enjoyed munching on oat grass when we had it available; but he never missed an opportunity to escape under the gate fencing when I wasn't looking to go munch on a bit of fresh green grass from the tiny yard outside the condo. I would then have to put him in a twenty-minute puke period before letting him come back inside to avoid having yet another present to clean up.

Max was also the best lap cat you could want. As soon as I settled into my chair to watch a little TV, he would spot me and jump into my lap. He would spin around a few times and settle in. He had this incredible grin on his face while I petted him. He'd lift his head so I could rub his neck, and his little motor would start purring.

Max's favorite toy was a laser. One Christmas, he got a bunch of toys: catnip mice, feathery boas, fake butterflies on a stick… you name it; but he got bored with most of them quickly. Once I took out the laser beam and shone it on the carpet, he was hooked. He would crouch down and get into predator mode. He would lift his hind quarters, his tail moving a mile a minute, then start making a little chirping sound while his eyes focused on the beam. Then he'd pounce on that dot like it was an alien invasion. I would shine the beam up the wall, along the couch, back on the floor, and all the while Max would be determined to catch the little bugger. Eventually, he would tire out and just plop down on the carpet and snooze. Those were fun times.

After many wonderful years, his health deteriorated to a point where his quality of life was at stake. One of the hardest decisions I ever had to make was having him put down. They say you never really get over the loss of a child. Even though he was a cat, Max was still my child, a big part of my life, and a loss I will never forget. He was part of my family for a long time, and he will always be loved and remembered as one of my own. I keep photos around to remind me of that love. Rest in peace, Max.

Dead Lights and Memories

It was December 21st, and I wandered in from work as usual. The house was dark, with the exception of a small kitty night light sticking out of the wall socket in the entryway. A whole seven watts of warm light lit up the area, just enough to slip off my shoes next to the door. I sprinted up the stairs, walked over to the dividing wall and flicked on the switch to turn on the Christmas tree lights. I took off my jacket and flung it over the chair, hung my car keys on the hook and reached over to the counter light switch.

The cats greeted me with their usual late afternoon demands for food, water and attention—in that order. Gus would usually jump up on the garbage pail and wait patiently for me to open a can of Friskies shreds with gravy. I pulled the tab and lifted the lid. Gus reached out his paw, letting me know he wanted to lick the lid, so I obliged him. Once he had it thoroughly cleaned, he jumped off to assume his feeding position next to the counter where his bowl would go.

I doled out their portions and set their dishes down. Samantha meowed—or should I say, screeched—nonstop until I set hers down. I walked back into the living room, grabbed the TV remote, hit the mute button and found the channel that showed *M*A*S*H*. My attention was diverted, though, as I looked at the string of dead white lights about halfway down the Christmas tree. "Oh great," I mumbled to myself. "Just what I need—an episode of "find the stupid dead light bulb" that decided to end its life four days before Christmas. So, I went over to the tree and started flicking at all the darkened lamps, hoping one might pop back to life so the world would be bright again. I flicked this one and flicked that one, but with no success. Finally, I remembered there was a fuse at the plug end, so around the tree I went, searching through the green branches and green wiring and eventually I found the plug.

Carefully unplugging it from the other strands, I slid my fingernail into the slot that contained the fuses and pulled it open. I popped out the two glass fuses and inspected them in front of the living room lamp. Sure enough, one was blackened. All I had to do was figure out what I did with the spare bulbs and fuses after I had put up the tree. I remembered it was a small, plastic baggie with the extra parts in it, so it might have been with the Christmas wrapping paper in my bedroom closet.

I flung open the double mirrored doors and pulled out the huge box of wrap. I dragged it into the bedroom and started going through the dozen or so rolls of brightly colored paper. I couldn't quite reach the bottom, so I dumped the entire box out onto the bed. Rolls of paper went flying, and some of them unrolled themselves right onto the floor. After rummaging through the mess, the spare bulbs were not to be found. I went back to the closet, pulling out this box and that box searching for that tiny bag of bulb parts when I accidentally dropped a cigar box full of old family photos.

I bent down to pick them up, and one photo caught my eye. It was an old black-and-white of a very dapper looking thin woman wearing a pantsuit, frilly blouse and a thin belt around her waist. I didn't recognize the person or the picture; and I wondered who it was and how it got there in the box. I quickly glanced at it again, then turned it over to see if there was a description of who it was.

The only thing written on it was a date: May 1944. I turned it over once again and studied the details. The woman was standing next to what looked like a World War II monument of a man on a horse. Behind it was a

stone building with white, small-paned windows along its front. At the bottom of the statue was a wreath propped up on a three-legged wire stand, adorned with an American flag ribbon around it. In the center of the wreath was a plaque of some kind, but it was too small to see what was written on it. I kept staring at the photo, hoping to find more clues, but I was getting nowhere. I hit upon the idea of enlarging the photo on my printer.

Since I had never done this before, I started pushing buttons on the machine, hoping to find the right combination of instructions on how to make something larger. After ten or so attempts, I finally found the solution. Push this button, use the drop-down menu and select another button. Arrange the photo on the glass, close the lid and hit the copy button. I quickly laid the photo face down on the glass and closed the cover. I pushed the buttons one by one, and the machine came to life. I heard the printer spring into action, its mechanism moving back and forth. I waited. I started to see the paper emerge from the exit slot. When it finally stopped, I grabbed the paper and turned it around.

I took it over to my desk lamp and glanced down at the sign on the wreath. *To the brave men who served in the Merchant Marines, from Battalion Station 924 on the USS McHenry, we salute you and your hometown of Carthage, New York.* I put my hand up to my mouth and gasped slightly. This was my mother! I glanced down at her left hand and noticed a very small diamond ring. Although I didn't know much about my mom before my birth, I did find out some things about my dad, and this photo kind of filled in a lot of the missing puzzle pieces of their young life together.

You see, my dad met my mom while on leave with the Merchant Marines in Jersey City. Mom worked in the Works Projects Administration (WPA), which was an eight-year program President Roosevelt initiated in 1939. The program employed mostly unskilled men and women to carry out public works projects, such as building hospitals, installing sewer drains, building bridges and planting new trees. Women in the program were selected to work in clerical jobs, gardening, canning, and as seamstresses for sewing projects.

I learned from an aunt that mom was really good at canning vegetables in jars, so she was probably put to work at one of the many soup kitchens that were built to feed a lot of the people employed by the government. My dad, on the other hand, was a cook while in the service. While on leave, with the ship in dry dock, the cooks would help out in the soup kitchens to aid in the government-sponsored work programs. I don't know the exact date they met or started dating, but I do know that Dad's hometown was Carthage, New York, he was stationed on the USS McHenry, and he got discharged from the Armed Services in April 1943.

When I got back to the living room after my recollection, I saw that Gus had jumped up on the fireplace mantel and knocked over a stuffed Abominable Snowman figure. There behind it was the missing package of spare lights and fuses. The Christmas tree lights got fixed on December 23rd.

Up on the Roof

We moved from a small house in Middletown, New Jersey, to a bigger house in Hazlet in the spring of 1959. The house was pretty nice, but the front yard was just dirt and a crabapple tree. The backyard was covered with a variation of beach sand. Since my father owned a landscaping business, it wasn't long before he got his crew to put down a nice blanket of fresh green sod on the grounds. Along with the grass, he planted a peach, pear and apple tree in the back yard. Once the trees were established, which took about two years, he sliced a large limb off the peach tree and grafted it to a sliced limb of the apple tree.

I watched him as he doctored the tree by using honey, sealing wax and a couple of powdery chemicals. The limbs were wrapped in bandage gauze and then painted with brown paint. I asked dad what he expected to happen, and he replied that he was testing out a new fruit he would call a *peachel*. I kind of snickered to myself, but didn't let on that I thought he had completely lost his marbles. Granted, my dad was a whiz at a lot of things, but trying to coerce a couple of fruit trees to produce misaligned fruit was too much to expect.

It took another two years before the trees bore

fruit, but the peach tree limb of the apple tree just simply rotted away and fell to the ground. Worms got to the ripened apples before the kids did, and there was hardly enough of a decent crop to make a small apple pie. So much for his wizardry in the garden.

The crabapple tree in the front yard grew incredibly big and tall in those first four years. In no time, I was able to climb up to the top, and that top limb was a good thirty feet from the ground. I loved climbing trees, and I really enjoyed just sitting up there among the branches and greenery, camouflaged from the somewhat hectic world below. I would spend hours watching the birds and clouds, or just closing my eyes and listening to the gentle wind rustle through the leaves. Occasionally, one of my siblings would seek me out and go squealing to the adults that I was being weird again by nesting in the crabapple tree.

In the spring of 1962, a song came out by The Drifters called *Up on the Roof*, and after hearing it for the first time I was inspired. No more crabapple trees for me. I eventually graduated to the roof. I fashioned a small step ladder out of discarded two-by-fours and climbed up on the shed in the back of the house. From there, I would gain my footing on the upper track of the window ledge and hoist myself up over the gutter onto the roof. I learned the hard way that wearing my Keds sneakers was much safer than wearing school shoes.

Once up there, I would walk up to the peak and straddle the apex of the roof. There I would sit with my back up against the cement chimney and watch the

not-so-exciting world below on Mason Drive. On some partly sunny days, I would lie on the warm shingles and just look up at the clouds, letting my mind wander. The good thing was that since no one could find me, no one would squeal on me. Oh, to be a kid again and to experience the simpler things in life.

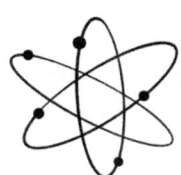

Measles Galore

I was around seven years old when the measles struck our house. One by one, the kids started showing signs of the infectious disease, and before you knew it we all had the classic blotchy skin rash, fevers and the red swollen eyes. For the better part of two weeks, all the kids looked like Disney-animated cheetahs with hundreds of tiny red dots. Since a vaccine wouldn't be developed until sometime in 1963, we had to let the virus take its course. Mom didn't know anything about the treatment, and the *Encyclopedia Britan*nica wasn't much help, either.

Once the third kid got it, Mom called our family physician, Dr. Charles H. Rothfuss. He lived about a quarter-mile away in Port Reading, NJ. Back then, doctors made house calls. He showed up sometime that evening and came upstairs to each of our rooms to take a look. Not much was known about the disease, but the good doctor suggested that we all band together in one room so as not to spread it around.

We started moving beds and linens into the master bedroom. The windows were covered with sheets to prevent more light coming in, which could cause the rash to intensify. The rash was really, really itchy, and we all had to wear our winter mittens so we wouldn't

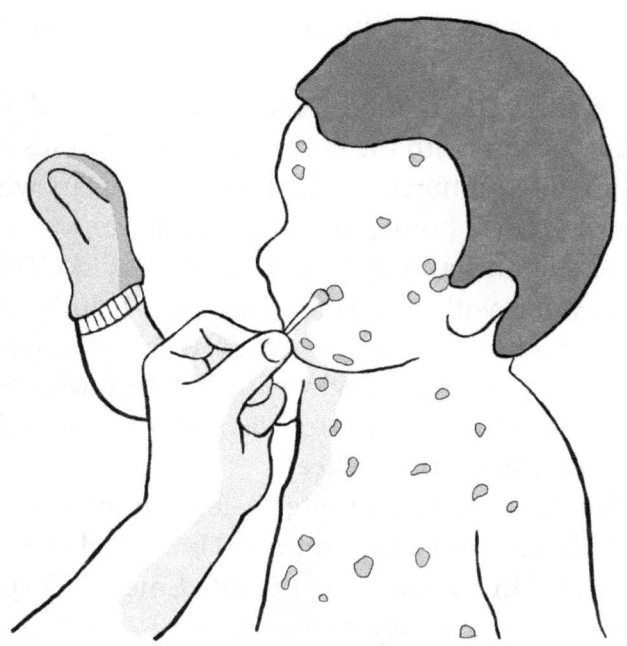

keep scratching ourselves and make it worse. Since our appetites were also affected, we got to eat lots and lots of broth and Jello. Each night we were slathered with calamine lotion, a beige colored ointment that smelled like kerosene. We were left to stand in our underwear until the stuff dried on our skin like plastic cement. We were only allowed to sleep in sheets—no blankets—and the room was kept quite cold.

Once each of us showed signs of healing, mom would take us by bus to visit Dr. Rothfuss at his house, just to be sure we were cured. He and his wife lived in a huge house with more rooms than I could count. They had a very large wrap-around front porch with its roof held up by five or six round wooden columns. He had his own laboratory set up in one of the downstairs rooms right off the examination room where he saw patients.

I wandered in there just to look around while Mom was busy with the doctor. He had all kinds of lab equipment, test tubes, beakers and rows of jars with all sorts of strange body parts in them. There was a full-sized skeleton standing in the corner. The skull's head was covered with a German Nazi war helmet with a feather sticking out of the side. On the other side of the room were small cages with live tiny white mice in them. One anxious critter was spinning around and around on an exercise wheel.

The doctor came in after a few minutes and did a quick once-over exam on me. He looked down my throat and in my ears, then handed me a red sucker. I remember mom paying the doctor $2 for the office visit and thanking him before we left.

When all the kids eventually got over the dreaded measles, we had to go back to school. If it weren't for the itchiness of the rash, I would have enjoyed it more because it gave me time to read my *Weekly Reader* magazines and my never-ending stash of comic books that people would bring over for us.

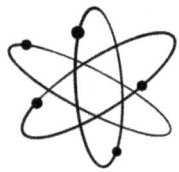

This "Z" Was Not for Zorro

In September 1962, I started my freshman year in high school. Like most of the other students, I was overwhelmed in the beginning with schedules, meeting new kids and learning to adapt to a whole new lifestyle in a new school. Like the others, I had to take general academic classes, such as science and math. I was assigned to Mr. Albert Kalme's first period math class, which started right after home room attendance.

Mr. Kalme was a man of about 40 years old, tall and pale. He spoke very slowly with a slight German accent. He had lost most of his hair at that age, and what was left was a distinct and rather unflattering comb-over. He wore mostly plaid suits with a dingy white shirt and drab, colored bow ties. On the first day, he introduced himself to the class. There was nothing unusual in his personal life that he cared to share with us.

Math was my worst subject, and the fact that Mr. Kalme's personality and teaching methods were equally as boring made for a long and tedious first period class. In the first few weeks, none of the kids in my class engaged Mr. Kalme in any meaningful conversations, other than the usual math-related queries. By the same token, he didn't care to participate in getting to know any of us. He pretty much kept to himself.

One day, during his class, I had trouble grasping the concept of quadratic equations and decided to linger after class to get some help from Mr. Kalme. At exactly 9:00 am the bell rang. The kids started gathering up their books, and within a minute everyone was gone except him and me.

He stared at me with a puzzled look, and finally asked if there was something he could help me with. I approached his desk, and as I did, he started erasing

the blackboard with his back toward me. Suddenly, I noticed something about him that I hadn't seen before. There, on the back of his head was a small square patch of bald skin that was noticeably discolored and showed the remains of what looked like stitches in the shape of the letter "Z".

Having grown up with many siblings, I've noticed all kinds of scars and stitches, but never anything like that. To say the least, I was intrigued; but I wasn't sure I wanted to inquire about it, either.

As Mr. Kalme turned around, my gaze turned away from his scar and I started to ask about my math dilemma. "You are curious about my disfigurement, Mr. Ricci," he blurted out in his staunch German tone. "It's perfectly good," he said. "You want for an explanation, yah?"

Well, now that the subject was raised, I was even more fascinated in knowing its history. What he revealed next was so riveting and thrilling, it has stuck with me all these years.

"I was a mere lad of 20 when the Germans invaded our small Polish village of Lublin. My father died when I was only 11, and my mother and I emigrated to Poland from Russia shortly after his death. I was an only child, and I was home schooled for most of my childhood. Mother was highly educated and worked at a nearby college teaching remedial physics to undergrads.

My passion was for math, and according to my mother, I was a child *protégé*. It came so easy for me, and early on I knew I wanted to focus on it as a career.

After graduating middle school, I enrolled in a nearby college, studying advanced mathematics and applied physics. A few of my colleagues and I started doing experimental studies in the field of cryptology. This was an exciting arena for our budding mathematical minds. We soon learned of the Germans' Enigma machine; and before long, all four of us were recruited by the infamous Polish Cipher Bureau to help decode the German messages.

"After the occupation of Poland, my friends and I were taken and held as prisoners. During my interrogation, it was revealed that my highly evolved math skills could become a very valuable asset to the Nazis. My friends were beaten and tortured, and they were forced to use their intelligence to help with the Nazis' plans to dominate Europe. I refused to help.

After spending many days in a German prison cell, I still did not give in to their demands. At times, the guards would corner me, taunt me and crush their lighted cigarettes out on my bare skin. At other times, they would insult me, mock me and playfully cut parts of my body with their very sharp bayonets. One night, I was summoned to appear in front of a high-ranking German official and given one last chance to cooperate. Again, I refused and was taken to a nearby hospital, where they informed me that I was going to get a frontal lobotomy in my brain. I was given anesthesia, and they were about to start the surgery when a bomb blast went off outside the hospital.

During the chaos, the resident doctor decided I wasn't worth the time or effort to do the intended surgery; so instead, he grabbed a small circular saw, cut a chunk of bone out of the back of my skull, installed a thin metal plate and sewed the skin back up with the signature swastika emblem. I was spared. Months later, the Allies invaded Poland. Those who had the opportunity fled to America."

Needless to say, I was stunned by what I had just heard; and in that moment, I just wanted to reach out and hug this brave and courageous man. I understood why he would not want to share that story, but I am glad he did. Mr. Kalme was a brilliant math teacher, but just knowing that little bit about his life made me respect him a whole lot more. To be that close to death and defy those odds had to be one of the most challenging things any human could possibly endure. To this day, whenever I see an oversized letter "Z", I don't think of *Zorro* like most kids. I think of my incredible math teacher, Mr. Kalme.

See Dick Run

I think I was about five or six years old when I met Dick and Jane. Like most kids growing up in the '50s and '60s, the fictitious family with oddly simplistic names would be a daily introduction to the world around us.

Apparently, some wise old philosopher decided that the correct teaching method for inspiring young minds could be taught by using phonics—sounding out simple one or two syllable words. Coupling these simple words with everyday experiences would also promote literacy with these young thinkers. And so, I was introduced to the Dick and Jane family. There was the young boy and his sister, and their baby sister, Sally. They also had a little pet dog named Spot. Interestingly, their parents and grandparents were nameless. They were just referred to as Mother, Father, Grandfather, etc.

They lived in a very simple house in Nowheresville on an unnamed street in an unnamed state. Father worked at an office somewhere in Nowheresville, and mother tended house. Although Father mowed the lawn on weekends, they did have a gardener, who, unlike the rest of the very white family, was a shade darker than the rest. Dick and Jane were very boring kids. They never fell down or broke an arm or leg. They had exactly four toys: a ball, a toy plane, a wagon and a sled; but these toys seemed to last them about five years, because they were never stolen by any other kids from school or in the neighborhood.

These kids never threw eggs at houses on Halloween, and never cursed or talked back to their parents or teachers. They never got mad or angry, and always went through every day with a smile. Even when baby Sally upset them, they always laughed it off as if she were royalty. I absolutely hated them!

I think what I hated most about them was that everything they said was conveyed in five words or less. "See Dick. See Dick run. See Jane. Jane has new shoes. See Sally. Sally sees a yellow car. Jane has my aero plane." In my world, if Jane took *my* aero plane, she would probably be bleeding. The problem was that

even when Dick ran, he never tripped on his stupid shoelaces or fell into a puddle of mud like a normal kid would. Oh, and you would never see Sally walking around with a nice round lump of poop in her diaper because Mom was too busy on the phone dishing gossip with members of the ladies' auxiliary.

Dick and Jane's nameless father was probably one of the least paid people in his office. You could tell because he always wore the same ugly brown suit and pale-yellow shirt with that equally offensive polka-dotted bow tie. It's apparent that he never helped his wife in the kitchen with the dishes, nor did he even once throw on a pair of sweats to engage his kid in a game of catch. This probably wouldn't have made a difference in the boy's life, since in every single book all this simple-minded kid knew how to do was run.

Week after week, when a new book was introduced, I couldn't wait to see if Dick was going to go absolutely berserk and maybe pee on the tree in the back yard. Maybe this week, Jane would finally steal her mom's nail polish, paint up all ten of baby Sally's fingers and toes, and dress up the kid to look like Miss Kitty from *Gunsmoke*.

Every situation in Dick and Jane's life was pure. Not once did their dog Spot come home covered in stench from fighting with a skunk. There was never an instance where Mother was so mad at Father that she broke each and every four-iron in his golf bag and threw the whole mess into the outdoor pool. Life was so peachy clean that even the gardener never complained to his boss that his kids had to be bused to a school clear across town.

Year after year, Dick and Jane did everything just right. They were, in fact, America's most perfect siblings. I would have loved for them to come live with my family of 11. I would have loved to see how they would cope in an overcrowded four-bedroom house with one bathroom and one TV. I'm pretty sure good old Dick would up and run away.

I often wonder what ever became of Dick and Jane. Did they ever leave Nowheresville? Did Dick go to college on a track scholarship? Did Jane wind up selling ladies' shoes at a Florsheim store? Did Sally eventually become the owner of a fleet of shiny new yellow taxis, or did she end up a dancer at some floozy night club? I guess we'll just have to just wait for the movie.

Goombas

If it was Saturday evening at our house growing up, you could almost always expect a weekly poker game there. Unless there was somebody's wedding to attend or a first communion, confirmation or baptism, there was a poker game. Dad would set up the card table and chairs in the den, get out the poker chips, a money tray, and arrange the buffet table with paper plates, wine glasses and ash trays. Around 6 pm, the *goombas* would start to arrive. In Italian cultures, the *goombas* were guys who could be family, but could also be business associates or just friends of friends. One by one, they came through the door, hung their long khaki-colored trench coats on the coat rack by the door, plopped their fedoras on a nearby chair and headed right into the den. My dad would greet the fellows with a big giant bear hug and a handshake. There would also be pats on the back and air kisses on each cheek. Once there were more than two, the loudness began. And these guys were LOUD! Between the many hand-gestures and the F-bombs, you could hardly make out a single intelligible word. Some of the men were right off the boat and would speak in broken English.

The poker parties weren't only about winning a

few hands of blackjack, although some of these hard-headed wops were pretty sore losers if they didn't win a hand in three rounds. There was lots of swearing, and sometimes a flattened hand could be seen being bitten on by their teeth. This gesture was surely one of the worst that could be thrown against a rival card player, for it meant *You'd better watch yourself, Mister!*

After a few dozen hands, Dad would call for a break and he'd whistle for a few of my older sisters to bring in the food. They would lay down a plastic checkered tablecloth so that the green felt on the table wouldn't get smudged. Then trays of cold cuts, cheeses, cut-up fruit, olives, hoagie rolls and a big jug of cheap guinea red wine would be brought out. A regular free-for-all would commence. After the first glass of wine, the conversations would get more personal. This would be when the guys shared hunting stories, wife and kid troubles, and who might be the next in line to get whacked. For those who were still single, breaking bread would be the perfect time to boast about the dates they had with the bimbo down at Uncle Tucci's Tavern or the well-sculptured simpleton waitress at Carmine's Pizzeria.

I can remember one of these card game nights when I was having trouble sleeping,, and since the noise downstairs was more interesting, I decided to descend the stairs to have a look see on my own. I peeked into the open doorway and the guy seated closest noticed me and nodded for me to come in. The smoke was thick and smelly, but my curiosity urged me to investigate. There I stood in my onesie pajamas next to Vinnie

"Boom-Botts," one of my dad's gun shop patrons. Right there on the table next to his piles of chips and cash was a bright, flashy Colt 45 handgun. I couldn't take my eyes off it. Finally, Vinnie picked it up and handed it to me. "Take it!" he said. "Not to worry, kiddo. It ain't loaded!" Damn, it was heavy! I just stood there with it wondering if this Vinnie guy had ever off'ed someone with it. "Thanks, Mister," I said. I placed it back up on the table and started to turn away. Vinnie picked up one of his bills and tucked it into my pajama top. "This C-note is for you, young man. Buy your mutter some flowers or sumthin' nice." I just turned quickly and ran back upstairs. Once in my bed, I slowly reached into my pajama top and pulled out the bill. I had never seen a $100 bill before, and it really made me nervous that I could possess something so valuable. I ran over to my closet, pulled out my Sunday shoes and stuffed the money into the toe of the right shoe. I knew it would be safe there.

The next morning when I came down to breakfast, I stopped by the den to survey the remnants of the mess from last night's gathering. My mom and sisters were sorting poker chips, vacuuming and putting away stuff. I wanted so much to tell someone about the money, but I was afraid they would take it away and use it to pay the electric or gas bill, so I kept quiet.

About four months later, I started getting cards from some relatives congratulating me on my first Holy Communion. One of the cards was from an aunt I had never seen before, and when I opened the card a brand-new, crisp one-dollar bill fell out. The card was not signed and there was no return address. All that was written on the card was, *To Junior. Congratulations. Go buy yourself something special.* Before my mother could ask who it was from, I ran upstairs and tore open my closet door. I grabbed my shiny new Sunday school shoe, pulled out the C-note and placed it in the card. I put the dollar bill in my sock drawer. I ran back downstairs and showed the card to my mom. "WOW!" she said. "It looks like you can buy that brand-new bike you've been wanting from W.T. Grants. It's a shame I can't send a thank you note to your aunt to thank her because I don't know which one it was." All I could say is thank God we have such a huge Italian family, including all the *goombas*.

The Re-Ak-Ner

My brother-in-law, Andy, was a rather unusual guy. He was a mixture of Irish and English with blonde hair and fair skin. Andy was young when he went into the Army. He served in Vietnam as a special communications operator. He was well educated, and his knowledge of electronics and mechanics served him well in the service. He met my sister, Lenora, just before he went into the Army; and they were head over heels in love with each other. To be quite honest, Andy had issues… lots of issues. I was usually on the receiving end of the sometimes-weekly crisis call from him. I used to call him Charlie Brown because for as long as I'd known him, he had this black cloud hovering over his head. He was always in a panic or crisis about something in his life, and I was his usual go-to life raft. I didn't mind being there for him when he needed to vent, as it brought us closer together—almost as much as my biological brothers did.

On those nights I would get the "Andy in distress" calls, I wouldn't hesitate to meet him for coffee, and we would sit like two old college buddies and shoot the breeze. Our favorite place was the Red Oak Diner on Highway 35 in the town of Hazlet, NJ. This was a typical Greek-owned place that was open 24 hours a day.

It not only served the usual burgers, fries and shakes, but lots of Greek specialties. You could also count on them to have a great selection of pies swirling around in their circular, refrigerated pie display.

You couldn't miss the place. Out by the highway, there was a huge metal sign in the shape of an oak tree with huge, red neon lighting in script spelling out the name RED OAK DINER. Even on the foggiest of nights, you could see the sign about half a mile away.

Andy and I spent many nights there in a back-corner booth near the window overlooking that huge sign, chatting about all kinds of things. We both loved talking about model trains, oldies records, stereo equipment and hot rods.

On one of those nights, our conversation got pretty serious. Andy confided in me about something very personal going on in his life: his marriage. He told me how he thought he was a failure and that he couldn't hold onto a decent job. He confided in me about not being able to provide all the things his wife and kids needed, and how he might have to go on a state assistance program just to make ends meet. I got pretty quiet and just sat there listening to him while staring out the window.

I couldn't offer much advice, except to say that I understood and cared about the dire situation he was in. Then he said something very unexpected. He said he wanted to get a divorce. I looked up from my coffee cup, looked him right in the eyes and said, "What?" He bowed his head and I turned to look out the window. Suddenly, the large bright neon letter "D" in the word RED started to flicker. It blinked and flickered on and then off, then on again. Andy had not said another word and I just kept staring at the sign. It flickered once more, then it just died out. I didn't think much of it at the time, but I think the "D" burning out was some sort of sign that he should end his marriage by getting a "D"ivorce. He didn't!

Months went by without a single distress call. I would pass by the diner once in a while at night, but the neon letter "D" never got fixed. Andy was working as a DJ, spinning records and making a decent living. Things were looking up for a while, and he and my sister Nora were finally seeing some light at the end of the long, dark tunnel.

One night, after working at a club in Bordentown NJ, he was on his way home when his old beat-up Ford Country Squire wagon broke down on the highway. It came to a stop along the shoulder, so it wasn't in a traffic lane; but the beast was dead. Andy pulled out an old army blanket, placed it over his milk crates filled with his prized record collection, then set out to hitch a ride home.

The next day he called me at work and explained what happened. I offered to pick him up after work and take him to get his car. Later that evening, we drove to his car. Luckily, it was still there on the side of the road. I pulled my car in front of his and got out my jumper cables. The car started right up. Andy asked if he could keep the cables in case this happened again, and I said it was okay. He walked to the back of his station wagon to open the liftgate and noticed that the entire back end was smashed in. Someone had hit the car and driven away. We noticed headlight glass on the ground, along with red plastic taillight lens pieces all around. Andy started to panic, and when we finally got the liftgate opened, his worst nightmare came true.

His entire collection of very rare and expensive oldies were smashed beyond belief. There among the broken milk crates were fragments of rare copies of the Duprees, the Danlieers, Fats Domino, and a hundred or more '50s and '60s records. "My Oldies!" he cried. "My prized collection is gone! It's taken me twenty years to build, and now it's all gone!"

I was at a loss for words to console him at that moment, but I did manage to ask if he had insurance. He just lowered his head and said no. I felt so bad for Charlie Brown. The following night, he called and asked if we could meet for coffee and chat. We got to the Red Oak about 7:00 pm.

We walked into the diner and sat in our same rear booth next to the window and started talking. Andy explained that he had met a guy who was willing to buy about fifty of his rare records that weekend, but now that income was lost. He needed that money to get caught up on his rent. He was almost in tears. Once again, I stared out the window and looked up at the bright red neon sign.

Suddenly, the letter "O" in OAK started to flicker, then dim and flicker some more. In the next few seconds, it just died out. It didn't dawn on me at the time, but I think the "O" burning out was a sign that he should get out of the "O"ldies record business. I wrote him out a check for his rent. I passed by the sign a few times in the following weeks, and the letter "O" was never repaired.

Andy had gotten a job working for New York Airways helicopter service based out of Newark, NJ. His job was mainly delivering lost or late arriving luggage to the travelers' homes. He loved this job because he drove mostly at night when there was little traffic, and he could also listen to his oldies in the car while making deliveries. In addition, the rich executives who took the copter back and forth to New York City would tip him very well when he showed up with their lost luggage. He had been working at New York Airways for about a year and a half.

One night, he was pulling out a large, oversized bag from the cargo hold of the copter. He underestimated how heavy it was. He twisted his body to keep it from falling out and felt something pop in his lower back. The light discomfort became worse, and the following day he could hardly move. After taking a medical leave from work, it was finally revealed that he had a slipped disc. He was put on disability, and since it wasn't the fault of the airline, they refused to pay for his medical treatments. He had no choice but to go on unemployment. The injury took many months to heal. Aside from his welfare and unemployment checks, there was hardly enough money to keep up with his bills.

The next distress call came in about two weeks later. "Can we talk?" he asked me. We met the following evening and sat at our table in the back next to the window. While sipping on my coffee and listening to the latest trials and tribulations of my sad-sack brother-in-law, I glanced out at the large neon sign near the highway. Both the "D" and the "O" bulbs were still dead, and this time the "D" and the "I" letters in the last word were flickering.

On and off they blinked, finally fizzling to a halt, and they just died out. It didn't dawn on me at the time, but I think the two letters "D" and "I" were meant to spell out a pattern of good ol' Andy's life. My mind started running through some words that began with "D" and "I". Disability, discontent, distraught, distress, dismay… Andy had all these symptoms. Once again, I felt sorry for him and wrote him a check.

The following night, I drove past the diner and all I could see was RE AK NER. I started to laugh to myself.

The Red Oak Diner was now officially the RE-AK-NER and it would never, ever be called the Red Oak again. I told Andy that we could no longer go there because they ran out of letters to burn out. He just laughed and agreed. The next time we went there together to chat, we sat on the opposite side of the diner where there were no windows or street signs to look out at.

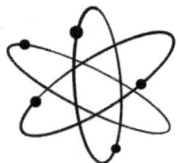

Dave and the Thirty Wandering Hens

Most of us at one time or another had one very special best friend. That friend was always there for you, and you were always there for them. They had your back, and they were the first ones to console you when things in your life went sour.

My friend David was all that and more.

I met Dave while working at a department store in New Jersey. I worked in the electronics department and Dave worked in small appliances. Our first encounter was a discussion we had about the quality of American made products as opposed to those coming from Japan and China. Back in the late '80s and early '90s, we were importing a lot of goods from East Asia, and this was putting a lot of American manufacturers out of business. Some of the imports were just plain crap, but some were far superior to anything made in the USA. Dave and I had many deep-hearted discussions about blenders, stereos, toasters and cassette recorders.

David and I were about the same age, somewhere in our mid 30s. He was about 5'7" and towered over my incredibly short 5'5" stature. While I am 100% Italian, David was a mutt, having the heritage of at least five different ethnicities. I had a rather typical Italian male build, broad shoulders, a tad muscular and a very prominent mustache which I had begun growing when I was 11. David was pale and skinny, and I'm sure he had to shop in the young boy's department for his clothes. Every shirt and pair of pants swam on him, and I can't remember ever seeing him without a pair of thick, loud-colored suspenders. Dave was also very witty, and every well-mannered barb I threw at him would be instantly returned with an equally abusive retort. We enjoyed sharing snide remarks at each other. I can't remember a time when we actually got mad at each other for something either of us said or did.

Since we both worked in the mall, we would meet at the food court for lunch and have a bite to eat. His go-to comfort food was a burrito. Mine was an Asian noodle bowl or a broiled chicken sandwich. We would often talk about family—mostly mine—as he was a brother to only one other sibling. I was part of a small army of nine loud and obnoxious Neanderthals. I guess he really wished to be from a bigger family, and I had always wished just the opposite. I was constantly entertaining him with stories of growing up poor and always having to go without something that other kids would take for granted. David's parents weren't rich by any means, but they provided him with the bare necessities. Anything over and above that he had to work and earn for himself.

David and I weren't the slightest bit athletic and we didn't care for contact sports. We both did enjoy bowling; and for such a skinny guy, Dave could throw a mean ball down the alley and throw way more strikes than I could.

I found out about him having ALS (Lou Gehrig's disease) unexpectedly during one of our lunch walks through the mall.

We were casually walking back to work when suddenly, David collapsed right in front of me. He went down slowly, as if he were a wooden puppet that someone had dropped its strings. Of course, I panicked and knelt next to him and started to question him. I sensed that he was completely embarrassed. He just asked me to pick him up and take him somewhere out of sight.

I didn't think twice and lifted him up in my arms. He was much lighter than I expected, and he felt like a larger-than-life Raggedy Andy doll. I carried him over to a wall where we sat down on a bench. While still on my lap, Dave looked up at me with big, brown, puppy dog eyes. He didn't need to say another word; he just sighed and thanked me. I had no idea what ailment he had, and I didn't want to speculate, so I waited for him to tell me.

I sat there in silence after gently putting him on the empty bench next to me. "I was born premature," he said. "According to my mother, an incident happened in the neo-natal unit when I was just two days old. I was given a short dose of nitrous oxide instead of oxygen. Luckily, they realized it quickly, but the doctors think it might have something to do with my neurological development. Most people get this when they're about 40 years old, but I started having symptoms at age 15. It doesn't happen too often, and I usually get a warning sign just before it occurs," he continued. It took me a little while for all of that to sink in. I just wanted to hug him and tell him that I understood what he was dealing with. I guess my first concern was him driving and what would happen if he got one of those attacks while behind the wheel. Since I didn't want to sound like his mother, I let it be.

I got a call from my friend, Jack, one late Saturday, asking me if I knew anyone who could cater a small dinner party for him. I asked him a couple of questions and told him I would get back to him. When I told Dave about the inquiry, he said, "Why can't you and I do it?" I do consider myself a pretty good cook, but I never thought of putting my talents to good use by catering parties. The more we talked about it, the more Dave convinced me we could certainly do this and make some decent money. The next thing I knew, we were planning a party for thirty guests, and the entrée of choice was herb-crusted Cornish game hens.

With the help of his mom and her kitchen, we prepared the hens, made a couple of fancy vegetable dishes, a few platters of appetizers and an Italian ricotta cheesecake for dessert. Since this was for a Valentine's Day-themed dinner, we used a lot of red veggies, tinted the cheesecake batter and topped it with fresh strawberries. The platters had heart doilies, and each chicken was adorned with paper hearts on a stick. We placed lots of little candy message hearts all over every serving tray and dish.

Finally, we had everything prepared and packaged, then put all the food on the back seats of his huge

Chevrolet Biscayne. The hens, all thirty of them, were packed in my very large stock pot with a heavy lid and tied with a large dish cloth fashioned into a handle. We drove over to Jack's house and started to unload the food to carry it to his kitchen. I took in the smaller trays of food first and then the desserts. As I was coming back out to the car, Dave had lifted the stock pot out from the back and grabbed hold of the side metal handles. I asked him if he needed my help and he said no. He started walking across the lawn to the house when the worst possible thing happened. He suddenly had one of his attacks, and down he went, along with the pot of chickens. The dish towel didn't hold very well, as the lid fell off and 30 small herb-crusted Cornish hens

went rolling down the very steep lawn onto the concrete driveway. I didn't know whether to laugh or cry.

I rushed over to Dave and lifted him up under his armpits. He was okay, though a bit shaken up and somewhat weak; but he managed to regain his strength within a few minutes. We just stood there in disbelief wondering how to save the day. I went over and picked up the stock pot. Luckily, there was a good three or four quarts of chicken stock left that hadn't spilled out. I quickly went to the car and grabbed a small kitchen trash bag and started collecting the chickens.

We got them into the house without anyone noticing the disaster. They rinsed off very well for chickens that were recently roughhousing on the front lawn. After warming up the juices and sprinkling lots of parsley all over each one of them, they were not only edible, but very eye appealing, as well. No one ever found out the truth, and the party was a success. That was the one and only catering job we did.

I eventually moved from New Jersey to Florida. The last I heard of David, he was working at Disney, chauffeuring VIPs around the park. After a few years of infrequent phone calls, we lost track of each other. I often think of David and the many good and bad times we shared, but I will never forget the story of the thirty wandering Cornish game hens.

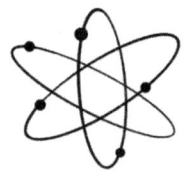

Jenny: The Cat's Meow

I put up an ad on the bulletin board at our local supermarket for someone to pet sit my cats. I put the usual information, such as how many cats, how often and what dates. I included paper strips with my phone number to tear off. A couple of days later, I started getting calls. Most of the people I chatted with were working full time or were retired and didn't drive. One gal sounded like she would be a good fit. Her name was Jenny, and she sounded like a genuinely nice middle-aged educated woman.

I asked a few questions about her previous experience with pets, and she assured me that she was very capable of handling my three little monsters. She asked me the names of my cats and I told her. She sounded extremely excited to meet them. I arranged for her to come over to my place the following Saturday.

Jenny arrived at 9 am sharp. They say first impressions are lasting impressions, and Jenny fit that saying to a "T."

She was definitely a middle-aged woman, about 5'6", 185 pounds, with glasses and long, black hair. She wore a very colorful panama straw hat with half a dozen small artificial flowers stuck to it, mostly posies. She wore a very colorful and loud orange and black pant suit with a large black belt around her waist. She had three different necklaces around her neck, one with a medallion of a lion's head. We introduced ourselves.

She walked up the set of stairs leading to our dining room and took a seat at the table. I offered her a beverage, and she asked if we had some strong coffee. I said that my Keurig was at the ready and it would only take a few minutes.

I had baked some lemon scones earlier, so we sat down to enjoy some fresh scones and coffee.

Jenny was outgoing and quite eager to chat. We discussed the usual things—where she lived, was she working or retired, what kind of animals she sat for previously, etc. I liked her. I liked her personality and her demeanor, and I didn't feel like there was anything I couldn't ask her. I asked if she was married, and she said she was. I asked about kids, and she said she had none. I asked her what she did before she became a full-time pet sitter, and she became outright silent.

She sat there and fumbled with some crumbs on the paper plate, sipped a bit more coffee, then finally looked up at me. "I worked on the phones at a call center," she said. "Oh," I said. "That must have been quite challenging!"

"You have no idea," she said. I paused and waited until she swallowed a bit more coffee, then she went on. "You see, I was on the receiving end of a booty call." I wasn't quite sure what she meant, so I nudged her to explain.

"I used to answer calls on a phone sex hotline," she

said, "And I was damn good at it, too." I nearly fell off my chair. The first thought in my mind was that this lady who was interviewing for a job as my pet sitter was so comfortable telling me that she used to be a phone sex solicitor.

How brazen, I thought, but how refreshing, too. Jenny began to go into detail about the calls and how she would entertain her clients with her varied number of different accents and her distinct flirtatious attitude. After describing a couple of specific incidences, I attempted to change the subject and offered her another beverage.

Jenny was certainly a different color apple in a rather mundane bushel of fruit. I hired her. She proved to be a really great sitter. She arrived on time, took great care of my kids, watered the plants, took in the mail, scooped twice a day and even brought the cats fresh catnip to munch on. I paid her well, and she had nothing but good things to say about her time with me and my cats.

About eight months went by and we were planning another short vacation. I called Jenny, but her number was disconnected. I called her husband's phone, and that number was disconnected. I called two of her previous clients that gave her references, and they hadn't heard from her, either. I sent her emails and kept phoning, but there was absolutely no response. It was if she vanished from the face of the earth.

To this day, it still remains a mystery what happened to my favorite pet sitter Jenny. She certainly was one person I will never forget.

Tuna, Coke and Cigarettes

Helen pulled up in front of Ocean TV and Appliances at exactly 9:15 am. She sat outside in her huge behemoth dark green Chevy Biscayne and honked the horn just as she did every day for years. I dropped whatever I was doing and went to get her.

Helen was in her early 70s, about five foot nothing and weighed probably as much as a bakery sack of flour. I pulled open her giant driver's side door, said a quick good morning, then reached in and took her by the arm. Helen then slid off the pile of cushions that her husband, Max, had fashioned for her so she could see over the steering wheel. Her seat was pulled up as far as it would go, and she still had about three inches between her and the wheel. Some days when it was a bit windy, I had to put my arm around her waist so she wouldn't blow away.

Once she was inside, she would slowly walk to her desk at the back of the store while grabbing onto things along the way to steady herself.

Helen was our in-store Gal Friday. She did some accounting work, prepared deposits, made our house call appointments, and generally answered the phone when my business partner, Elmer, and I weren't there.

Once she settled in, she had a routine that God

forbid anyone should alter. She would reach into her pocketbook and pull out a small Tupperware container. In it would be one hard-boiled egg (peeled and cut in half), a half stick of washed celery cut into exactly nine 1/8"-thick pieces, and three slices of peeled apple wrapped in Saran wrap. She would then hit the small round desk bell next to her lamp only once, and one of us would come to her aid. I was usually the one.

I put her Tupperware in the fridge and got her white plastic cup from off the shelf. I opened the freezer compartment and pulled out a tray of ice. We didn't have the luxury of an automatic ice maker back then. Once I had a few cubes loosened, I would place them in the cup and set it down in front of her. Then I would grab a can of regular Coca-Cola, pull open the tab and set it down next to the cup.

At this point, Helen had slipped out of her long blue fleece overcoat and motioned for me to hang it up. After she poured a bit of Coke into the cup, she would light up her first of about thirty Salem cigarettes that she would smoke that day. Finally, she would grab the remote control and fire up the small 9" Emerson television sitting on top of the fridge. She always set the dial to channel 4 so she could watch *General Hospital*. The volume would be muted until it came on; and when it was over, she switched to channel 7 for *One Life to Live*.

Helen didn't care for many other TV shows, but she did enjoy watching (but not listening to) Bob Barker on the *Price is Right*. Now that she was settled in, she took a sip of Coke from her plastic cup and took a long drag or two on her cigarette. Now she was ready to talk. "Grab the till, Ricky," she said, never once having called me by my first name. I didn't mind it. She was old, eccentric and set in her ways. I brought over the previous day's receipts, along with the cash drawer (we didn't own a cash register), and she proceeded to add, subtract and make entries in her ledger. She then handed me a bunch of repair call slips and the deposit. I began planning my day at the shop.

The store wasn't all that big. We sold some medium-sized color TV consoles, a few video cassette recorders, some portable radios, children's record players and some other small appliances. We took in repairs on just about anything that had a plug, and I did most of the in-store repair work. Elmer did the house calls. We had a really old Ford Econoline van

Tuna, Coke & Cigarettes

that sucked up gas like no tomorrow; but it served our purpose, and we didn't have to make payments on it.

Around 11:55 am, Helen rang the small, shiny bell on her desk. This was my clue to help her prepare her lunch. She set aside her *New York Times* Sunday crossword puzzle (that she did in blue ink), cleared off the bills and statements and laid down a fresh paper towel.

I came in and grabbed a small can of StarKist tuna off the shelf, pulled open the tab and removed the lid. Then she laid down three Krispy saltine crackers in a row. Next, she opened up her Tupperware and took out the celery slices, placed them down on the towel along with one half of the egg. She put the three ounces of tuna in her little bowl. With her fork, she smashed the egg into pieces and added a drop of mayo. She then mixed that up and divided it among the three crackers. Then she placed three slices of celery on top of them, poured more Coke into her cup, and lunch was ready.

Sometimes she would extinguish the burning cigarette and other times she just let it sit there while she ate as the smoke billowed up toward the overhead lamp until it burned itself out at the filter. On warmer days, I had to make sure to replenish her ice cubes and remember to refill the trays so she would never run out of cubes.

We paid Helen $40 a week (under the table) and supplied her with crackers, small cans of tuna, four six-packs of Coke and three cartons of Salem cigarettes a week. Our arrangement lasted the entire time I worked there, which was about four years.

Everyone in the strip mall knew and loved Helen.

So did we. She never called in sick and never complained about the heat or cold. Not once did she ask for time off to go on a vacation, and we never got audited by the State or the Federal government for discrepancies in our taxes.

Our TV sales and repair business was nearing its end when department stores started popping up at every giant mall and forcing small mom and pop places like ours out of business.

The owners of the strip mall started raising the rent, and we weren't selling or repairing enough to keep the place going. The business next to us, Automobile Association of America, wanted to expand their space, so we negotiated a buy-out with them.

After having a Going Out of Business sale, we closed up shop.

It was a sad day when I had to say goodbye to Helen, escorting her out to her giant Chevy and placing her in it for the very last time. I put a box containing her remaining Coca-Cola, saltines, tuna fish and cigarettes in the back seat, closed the door and stood by her side window. She was never the type to get emotional, but I was; and she knew I was all choked up over this.

She rolled down the window and lifted her arm up over the glass. She took my hand and stared into my face. I'll never forget her last words to me. "Yesterday was our beginning, today is our end; but somewhere in the middle we became good friends. Good luck in your next adventure, Lenny Ricky!" I waved goodbye as she sped out of the parking lot in her giant Chevy sedan.

For 40 Days and 40 Nights

Our family moved from a split-level house in Middletown, New Jersey to a newly constructed sub-division in a small hamlet called Hazlet in the spring of 1959. The houses were built by men who returned from the Korean war with minimal carpentry skills and had the ability to erect these homes in record time. We would find out later that the men skimped on some necessary construction requirements that would have prevented future mishaps.

Dad surveyed the property in the winter of 1958, shortly after the foundation was completed and the framing had started.

When we moved in, the back yard was just a mixture of beach sand and topsoil with not a blade of grass to be found. It's a good thing Dad was in the landscaping business. He planted a nice, healthy green mixture of Kentucky blue and rye grasses. It took about six months, but the backyard turned out great and it was a nice place for the large brood of kids to frolic and play.

Our first winter there was dreadful. Snow started to fall at the end of October and stayed on the ground well into the beginning months of spring. Every new couple of inches of snow just piled up and froze on the previous snows, and it never totally went away until the daffodils appeared in late April. Then the rains came. When it rains in New Jersey, it's an all-day affair. It could go on for a couple of days at a time, as well. Eventually, the melting ice, snow and rain would saturate the backyard. All that water had nowhere to go… except into our basement.

As the basement was just below ground, the builders had installed three corrugated metal window wells around them. If they were meant to keep out the water, they failed miserably. After the second day of rain, the window wells filled up with water and started seeping through the flimsy metal window frame and down the walls. Dad got a couple of his landscapers and a backhoe, then dug a trench to allow the water to flow from the yard into the street. That worked for a little while until the trench collapsed into itself from the heavy water stream.

Whenever we expected heavy rains, we just pulled the beds away from the windows and put down lots of beach towels to keep the water at bay.

A few years went by. Dad passed away, my three oldest sisters got engaged, married and moved out. I still lived in the basement and just dealt with the water issue whenever it came up.

One day, after another full day of rain, Mom casually walked down the stairs into the basement with her laundry basket with the intention of getting a load of laundry started. As she approached the second to the last step, she yelled for me to come downstairs. She sat down on the step, me hovering over her shoulder and we just watched in silence. The entire basement was flooded—my bedroom, the closet and the laundry room. Everything was drenched. Shoe boxes were floating; newspapers and books were drifting across the tiny waves. A now totally worthless Diana Ross and the Supremes record album was bobbing up and down in the water with no direction at all. Among the floating objects was a wooden clothes pin with a small family of black water bugs hanging on for dear life. They drifted out past the stairs and disappeared under the couch. A pair of flip-flops had found their way out of the closet and were inching their way into the laundry room.

Mom and I just stared at each other. I took off my shoes and socks and stepped down into the three or so inches of very cold water, surveying the disaster as I went. That's when I noticed the rather large split in the cinder block wall and the nicely formed stream of dirty water flowing from it into our home. Mom put down the laundry basket and followed me into the laundry room. The water level was just about up to the bottom of the water heater, so I turned that off. Luckily, the furnace was sitting a bit higher, so that was not in any danger.

As we waded through the cold and murky water, we came up with a plan. I reached up into an overhead cupboard and pulled out four woolen winter blankets and laid them down into the water. I gathered up a few small, discarded area rugs and threw them down. Once they were saturated, I lifted them into the Speed Queen washer and set the dial to Spin. Mom and I worked long and hard, lifting the soaked mops, blankets and rugs into the utility tub, squeezing out the water and popping them into the washer.

Little by little, the remaining water seeped out from under things and settled into a puddle in the center of the room. We toweled up the remaining water and picked up a few dozen dead creatures as well—mostly crickets, spiders, earthworms and a centipede or two. I did manage to rescue a tiny, green baby frog that came floating by on an empty PAAS Easter egg coloring kit box.

Once we were finished, we got out the box fans and

set them all to high, opened up the overhead windows and called it a day.

I tried installing sump pumps into the window wells, but that didn't help much. In the fall, they would fill up with tons of leaves and debris, which clogged the fan mechanism.

After about eight years of playing the flooded basement game, we finally realized that the construction people never did put a layer of hot tar along the foundation like they were supposed to. The constant freezing and thawing of the wall caused it to crack, which led to the damage. We eventually installed French drains in the basement. That didn't really solve the problem, but it was bearable until we sold the house twenty years later.

For Just a Dollar?

A visit to the dentist isn't on anyone's list of fun things to do, but since it's necessary, we make the best of it. I was sitting in the waiting room, watching the clock tick by. It was sometime in the late '70s. The table before me was laden with an assortment of old, thumb-worn magazines that looked like they had seen better days. Some front covers were missing, so you couldn't even make out the titles of the publications.

As I rustled through the stack, I came across a copy of *Rolling Stone*. I wasn't much into music, but this magazine looked more promising to read than *Jack and Jill* or *Catholic Nun's Monthly*. I started flipping through the pages, every now and then pausing to listen to the dental assistants announce the next victim's name. A short reprieve and I was back to flipping pages. Just then, an advertisement caught my eye. The ad showed a perky teenage gal with bouncy red hair holding a box of 8-track tapes. The headline above her shouted, *Go a little crazy. Get a lot of music... 11 records or tapes for just $1*. There, splattered on the page and the adjoining page, were listings of 60–70 titles of top name artists and their latest albums.

I couldn't believe what I was seeing. How could they sell you 11 8-track tapes for just a dollar? This must be a gimmick. My eyes wandered down to the corner of the page; and there, stuck to the bottom, was the magic post card that you filled out with your selections to mail it in. Even the postage was paid. WOW! I thought.

I quickly thumbed through my pants and shirt pockets for the little yellow bowling score pencil which I had stolen and always carried around with me. I looked around to make sure no one was looking, then tore off the post card. I started filling in the numbers of the selections for the tapes I wanted.

B25688—*The Best of the Fifth Dimension*... H42566—*The Mamas and The Papas Sing Monday Monday*... A77845—*Listen to the Music with the Doobie Brothers*... V32887—*My Sharona* by The Knack. By the time I got to my last selection, they called me in. I quickly stashed the post card in my pocket and followed the receptionist into the room of terror.

I dropped the post card in the mail slot at the corner drug store. A few weeks later, a HUGE package arrived.

Inside were all 11 of the 8-track tapes, wrapped in cellophane tape. I quickly ran up to my room and turned on my Radio Shack stereo and popped in a tape. After that one, then another and another. It would be a week later that I remembered I had to send in my dollar, or I would probably get a nasty letter from Columbia House. I searched frantically for the box, but to no avail. It must have gotten thrown out.

About two weeks later, a package arrived from Columbia House. In it was an 8-track tape of someone named Billy Swan with his Top 10 recording of *I Can Help*. "What gives?" I thought to myself. "I didn't order this." I tore into the enclosed envelope and found my answer. It read: "Here is your monthly selection. We hope you enjoy it. Your next selection of *The Best of Grand Funk Railroad* will arrive in three weeks." And in the tiniest of print: "Unless you send in the post card and check the box marked, *I do not want a selection this time*, please pay the enclosed bill to keep your selections coming."

I nervously tore open the envelope marked HERE IS YOUR BILL and almost fell out of my chair. There, in black and white, were my 11 selections that I got for a dollar, along with the bill for the shipping and

handling which amounted to $37.85. On top of that was the bill for the Billy Swan tape that I didn't order, including that shipping and handling which came to another $8.98. So much for getting a bargain.

I sat down and wrote a nice letter to the people at Columbia House telling them to cancel my subscription. That didn't happen. I kept getting more tapes and more bills and more bills after that. I finally got collection notices and threats of legal action. At one point, I think they were going to kidnap my younger brother and hold him ransom until the debt was paid. That didn't happen.

Mom's advice, after I spilled my guts to her, was that I should always remember that if something looks too good to be true, it probably is. Thanks, Mom. Now you tell me.

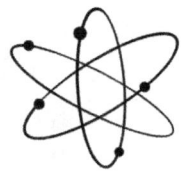

The Light Bulb Thief

For as long as I could remember, I liked celebrating my birthday as most kids do. Unlike most kids, I didn't just want a cake, a couple of friends over and a bunch of annoying adults belting out *Happy Birthday to You*. Instead, I went places. At first, they were quick trips to places I could get to by a short train ride or bus. If I was lucky enough to secure a large amount of birthday money, it meant a trip to the biggest, greatest and most elaborate toy store in all the world: FAO Schwarz in New York City.

If there ever was a toy a kid wanted, this store had it. It was five floors of heaven for a 14-year-old. I bought myself a huge tin-type Boeing 707 jet that took twenty batteries, had tons of green and red flashing lights and made lots of airplane noises. The entire plane spun around in a circle, lifted its wheels for takeoff and sped across the wooden floor for a good 40 feet before powering down. After five trips across the floor, the left wing fell off and exposed the tiny now-broken wires inside. There's $12 I would never see again.

Each year after that, I ventured a bit further away from home. I celebrated my birthday on the Atlantic City boardwalk one year and amassed an amazing 1,700 Skee-Ball tickets in less than an hour. I came home with a fancy pocket watch that ticked and tocked for about a week before I busted its main spring from overwinding it.

The following year, I took the Cape May ferry from the southernmost tip of New Jersey across the Chesapeake Bay to Lewes, Delaware. I found out the hard way that the beaches in Delaware were not very clean. They were chock full of horseshoe crabs and seaweed. I did manage to find a nicely formed dead starfish on the sand. I carefully tucked it away in a plastic soda cup with a little sea water for the ride home. Once home, I carefully took it out of the cup and placed it on my dresser. It was a great souvenir of my birthday trip to the beach until my cat Trixie discovered it and mistook it for her stuffed catnip mouse. The next day, I found the five missing starfish arms strewn all over my bedroom.

It wasn't until I was 32 years old that I re-visited FAO Schwarz in New York City. It was my birthday again, July 10th. My friend, Gene, and I drove into the city. While walking along Fifth Avenue, I came across my once-favorite toy store. Gene asked if I had ever been there. I told him the story of my birthday trip at 14 years old and of the giant airplane I had bought that day. I also told him that no matter what souvenirs I had brought home from my birthday trips, they all seemed to break or get lost or something. "Well, today you should get something to remind you of your birthday trip—a collectable," he said.

I thought about it for a while; and as we were riding the escalator, I hit on an idea. What if I stole a unique light bulb from every place I visited? I could write on them where I stole them from, the date I took them, and put them in a box to save. I didn't tell Gene about my idea, but once up on the second level, I went over to a string of bright white pointy light bulbs and unscrewed one. I stuck it in my pocket.

When I got home, I wrote on it, *Stolen from FAO Swartz Toy Store, July 1980*. Through three decades I stole light bulbs. I have one from the US Energy Exhibit at the 1982 Knoxville World's Fair. I have a small, orange Christmas-type bulb from the Taco Bell in San Diego from November 1994. I took a nice bright white one from a Bette Midler concert at the Suncoast Dome in St. Petersburg, Florida in the spring of 1994. I have a bright yellow bulb from Bo Jangles chicken place in Atlanta from July of 1989.

I have another cute orange one from the Snow-White Laundry in Long Branch, New Jersey from October 1988. In San Francisco, in December 1985, I took a cute little green Christmas light right off of a Christmas tree in a little card store called Does your Mother Know. I have another from TuTu's Café on the Road to Hana in Maui, Hawaii from June 2001. I think I stopped stealing them in 2004.

I took out my strange 85-piece collection from the top shelf of my bedroom closet a few months ago while collecting some things to give to charity. For about two hours, I sat there pulling one light bulb after another and reading all of the wonderful places I had been to in those three decades. It was sort of like reading a written journal, but my mind did all the reminiscing by

triggering the names of the places and where I was at the time. From restaurants to clubs to obscure antique shops from one coast to the other, I collected memories by stealing light bulbs. The interesting part about this whole story is that I never broke a single one. Of all my birthday treasures, they outlived the watches, the airplanes and the starfishes. Even though they're old and full of dust, I couldn't ask for a nicer way to remember my many outings than looking through my collection of vintage stolen light bulbs.

A Visit to the World's Fair

I was lucky to have visited the 1964-1965 New York World's Fair not just once, but three times. Living right across the river in New Jersey made it a quick bus ride to Flushing Meadows in the Queens section of the city.

My first visit there was in April 1964 with my two brothers. I was a mere lad of 15. The nation was still reeling from the assassination of President John F. Kennedy, and the world needed a place to just go and forget about that awful tragedy five months prior.

Admission was $2 and most of the exhibits were free. Major corporations like General Electric, RCA, Chrysler, General Motors, IBM, Bell Telephone, DuPont and Kodak had rides or stage shows, and some others charged a small admission to see special exhibits. I remember we paid 50 cents to get a peek at the actual sculpture of Michelangelo's *Pieta* from the Vatican Pavilion direct from Rome.

Walt Disney introduced the world to animatronics with his ride, It's a Small World. It featured robotic dolls from all nations dancing to a very catchy tune that you couldn't get out of your head for the rest of the day.

The central theme of the fair was "Peace through

Understanding", which was exemplified by the enormous stainless-steel model of the world called The Unisphere. Rising 140 feet high and weighing 700,000 pounds, it could be seen from anywhere on the grounds of the fair. If any one of us should get lost, we would get reunited at the globe.

One of the most memorable things I remember about the fair was seeing color television for the first time. Radio Corporation of America (RCA) had an actual studio there where you and your friends could go into separate rooms. The TV camera would record you live and beam you in blazing color onto the TV screen in another room. We were totally amazed by that. The production crew would first dress you in a red sport coat over your street clothes so they could emphasize the brilliance of their new COLOR broadcast system.

While walking through the many exhibits and displays, we came across the DuPont pavilion. On this particular day, they were having a "Best Legs at the Fair" contest. DuPont was joyfully introducing to the public their newest chemical creation called cantrece nylon. There, in front of the building, were twelve incredibly attractive young ladies in skirts, sweaters and high heels showing off their very curvaceous legs adorned in the newest of nylon stockings. Naturally, we stopped—like hundreds of others—and voted by writing the contestant's number on a slip of paper and dropping it into the ballot box nearby. We didn't wait to see who won, as there were so many other things to see and do.

Ford Motors introduced us to the very first Ford Mustang. Every young lad probably spent every dime of their savings to buy one after seeing it at the fair. Ford Motors had one of the best exhibits. The Disney Company and Ford got together and created a magic skyway ride where you sat in an actual Ford Mustang modified for the ride. It drove you around a series of dioramas that depicted the earth around the time of the dinosaurs.

The mood through the ride was dark and eerie, with cold steam pipes pushing vents of air in and around the robotic animals going about their day. Distant volcanoes spewing lava and ultra-large prehistoric animals making loud menacing sounds made for a very realistic experience. I often wondered what happened to those 76 modified Mustangs after the fair closed.

For all the amazing technological strides and advances in engineering, architecture and innovation, man's dream of a perfect utopia was no more evident than what was displayed at the General Motors exhibit: Futurama. It showed a promise of tomorrow where huge, barren, icy tundras were transformed into working habitats for growing communities. It touched on the vast, outer reaches of our solar system, where desolate planets could be made habitable by new technologies in agriculture and water purification. It showed great promise in the cities of tomorrow with moving sidewalks, jet propulsion vehicles with no traffic, and people living in floating structures made of fiberglass and lightweight metals.

As you moved further on, the immense oceans of the world were made livable by underwater housing units made of indestructible materials, where substantial amounts of minerals and ores were extracted to provide enough energy fuels to power the entire planet. Once you left this ride, you felt truly inspired that this would surely be the future you would live in. Too bad most of it won't be realized in our lifetime, but perhaps it can in our children's.

Another impressive invention was revealed to the world by the Bell Telephone System. It was called a picture phone. Picture phone was supposed to revolutionize the world and help bring people closer together. This is, of course, way before portable phones were invented.

The device was a simple 4" by 5" TV screen set in an oval metal box on a small stand. The telephone was connected to the back of the device with a wire. The phone was a standard princess phone desk model. The idea was that grandma could sit at her home in Schenectady, New York, dial up her grandson in Bakersfield, California, and the two would be able to see and hear each other as plain as day. Little Bobby could show Grandma the nice gash he got from riding his bike, which would surely prompt Gram to put a ten-dollar bill in a get-well card and get it in the mail. There would be no denying the pain and suffering if you saw it live.

As primitive as it was, it seemed like a good idea as long as every single person had a comparable device. They weren't cheap, and a three-minute call to

Grandma cost $16. That would be equivalent to $121 today. According to AT&T historian Sheldon Hochheiser, the video phone was "the most famous failure in the history of the Bell System." To be honest, I'm sure its failure wasn't just the cost of the unit; but also that nobody wanted to see their uncle George prancing around in his living room in his striped boxer shorts.

Among the many states and nations that exhibited booths and displays was one from Wisconsin that featured the world's largest hunk of cheese. My brothers and I weren't that interested in dairy products, so we skipped that. Florida's pavilion featured a dolphin show, flamingos and a talking parrot. We skipped that, also.

What young boy wouldn't want to spend time staring up at an actual life-sized model of a Saturn 5 booster rocket with a genuine Gemini capsule on top? That had to be one of the most spectacular sites I had ever seen, to be that close to something so significant in my time relating to the exploration of our very own solar system. The United States Space Park, sponsored by NASA, was one place I could have spent the whole day. I knew I had to make a return trip to the fair just to see all the other space stuff like the lunar rover, the Apollo service module and dozens of communications and weather satellites.

I guess my final memory of visiting the World's Fair was during my second visit to the fair in May of 1964. I got to see a man fly. It was mostly a publicity stunt, but I got to see Mr. Bill Suitor, AKA "Jetpack Man", perform a 20-second flight using a fuel propelled flying suit. I managed to get a great viewing spot right in front of the Court of the Presidents. Mr. Suitor pushed a trigger button he held in both his left and right hands.

A loud burst of compressed air spewed out at tremendous force along the pavement. Up he went, hovering above the crowd for a few seconds. He then proceeded to hop completely over the two rows of flags. Bill then took off higher into the sky, until he reached the giant Unisphere globe, where he flew in a circular path above the fountains below. He finally landed in a patch of grass across from the New Jersey pavilion. I, like many other youngsters at that time, imagined that in just a few years, everybody would be flying around in the air like super people, getting from one place to another in a fraction of the time it took to drive or take a subway. That didn't happen, either.

I have visited many other World's Fairs in my later years, but none compared to the magnificence of that one. It was said they didn't make much money on the fair after it finally closed, but for kids like me, it was worth every cent of my $2 admission. I would have gladly paid $3.

My Summer in Carthage

I got to visit my Grandma Ricci only one time growing up. She lived in Carthage, New York, and that was a pretty far distance from where we lived in New Jersey. I remember making the awfully long journey riding in the back of my dad's Ford Country Squire station wagon. It had huge windows in back. You could see both where you were going and where you came from by just turning your head a bit. The back door opened outward, making it easy to get in and out, and the window had a crank so you could adjust how much air you could get while still protecting you from sticking your whole head out and making funny faces at the cars behind you.

In the summer of 1960. I was a mere 12 years old. The trip was long and tedious, but luckily the New York state thruway was a smooth, paved highway. It wasn't until we exited and got onto local roads that the pleasant smooth drive turned into a prolonged rendition of rigorous bronco busting. Let's just say that after an extended cold and snowy winter season, it would take the highway department about eight months to finally patch up the hundreds of potholes that appeared once the snows melted. It was no fun being bounced around in the back like a demented dashboard bobble-head.

My grandparents lived in a rather large, two-story mid-century farmhouse on a tract of land that bordered a secondary line of the New York Central Railroad traveling between Utica and Carthage.

One of my favorite memories of visiting Gram was waking up in the middle of the night to the sound of a 100-plus car freight train passing right in front of the house. Since there was a paved road adjacent to her house, they had to blow the diesel horn 100 feet from the crossing. The bedroom where I slept was on the second floor, overlooking the front of the house. No sooner did I hear that whistle that I bounded from my bed and threw open the window. I would sit on the ledge in my PJs watching the approach of the giant locomotive. I loved counting the cars and trying to remember the many names of the different logos on the rolling stock.

My grandparents were fresh off the boat from Italy, and they spoke only broken English. Neither of them could remember any of their grandkids' names, so they numbered us. I was #5 for as long as I could remember. Gramps had a small dog, a chihuahua named Gigettha, that yapped incessantly and never left his side. It had a small collar with a bell on it that was equally annoying.

Whenever Gramps was not holding that dog, it was running amok around everyone's legs as if it were purposely trying to trip you. Gramps just laughed it off and yelled in Italian at the dog to stand down. That proved useless, as the animal had a boundless amount of energy that wouldn't wind down until after midnight. It also didn't know English, let alone Italian.

My dad presented his parents with a 30-year wedding anniversary gift: a black-and-white television that Gramps referred to as a light box. It was a huge beech wood cabinet that stood about 6 feet high and had a screen the size of a postage stamp. I can't ever remember Grandma watching it all during the time I was there. Unlike where we lived in Jersey, the folks up in the wilderness of New York State could only get two broadcast stations. One station was out of New York City and the other was from Albany. Luckily for me, one of them was WPIX.

I tried never to miss an episode of the *Andy Griffith Show* or *My Three Sons*, but watching them on Grandma's poor excuse for a television was a nightmare. If the set wasn't rolling horizontally, it was rolling vertically, and the sound would spit and sputter just as much as the picture. After a while, I gave up on that and just listened to music on my 8-transistor Arvin pocket radio. If I sat still long enough facing north, I could get through one entire playing of *Poor Little Fool* by Ricky Nelson with nary a single fadeout.

There was one very bizarre, but memorable, day for me while staying with Gram. I was playing in her back yard on the tire swing when she pushed open the back-screen door and yelled for me to come help. "*Il Numero Cinque! Viene qui.*" (Number 5, come here!) I slipped off the tire seat and ran to her. My Italian wasn't that good, but she mentioned *bisogno* and *pollo* in the same sentence. She tried saying it again with a little more English. "I need-a you to catch da chick."

"Oh," I said with enthusiasm. Next thing I know,

I'm running all around the back yard chasing a big, old, but very fast chicken. Gram just stood there with her billowing flowered apron, hands on her hips, watching me trying to outmaneuver the stupid barnyard fowl. After about ten minutes of me running around, falling down and getting back up from sliding in God-knows-what on the ground, I finally cornered the feisty chicken in a corner and grabbed her. She put up a pretty good fight, but I was spared with just a single peck on my hand. Gram, watching the entire spectacle, motioned for me to bring the chicken and to hold it next to a tree stump.

Lenny Ricci

Before I could react, down came an axe and off came the chicken's head, rolling off to the side of the stump. I was half in shock. I dropped the headless chicken, and off it went scattering all around the yard, spewing its innards and leaving quite a bloody trail. Gram started mumbling words in Italian faster than I could decipher them and eventually went over to the now motionless chicken and plucked it up.

A pot of boiling water was waiting in the kitchen. Grandma plopped the bird in the water as I cautiously watched from the kitchen door. She put the lid on the pot and walked away. The house smelled awful. I didn't stay to watch the rest of the preparation, but knowing this was going to be dinner completely turned my stomach. I do remember having a peanut butter and jelly sandwich that night.

I must admit, I did learn a lot about gardening from her, and even how to tie a necktie while dressing for church one Sunday; but aside from that, not much else. I managed to overcome my fear of dead chickens. I will still eat them, as long as I don't have to catch them and behead them. Some things are just better off store bought. That was the last time I saw my dad's parents.

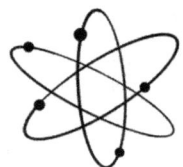

The Rain, the Park and Other Things

My good friend, Chris, was a super nerd. I met Chris while attending a vocational training seminar in early 1980. As two young men interested in the sciences, we spent a great deal of our free time watching VHS tapes that had to deal with geography, philosophy and science fiction. We both loved *Star Trek* and were constantly quoting both Mr. Spock and Captain Kirk. Most of our lengthy conversations on those topics were anything but "illogical," according to the science officer.

Chris and I loved learning about new technologies and innovations in engineering and science, but the trouble was that we had no one to share our enthusiasm with. Most of our family members were only educated through ninth grade and cared little about world affairs. When Chris and I first heard about the upcoming World's Fair in Knoxville, Tennessee in 1982, we decided to plan a trip. The fair's theme was going to be about energy and world peace, things we were both passionate about.

At the time, Chris was working at a Sizzler steakhouse restaurant, and I was working at a ceramic tile factory. Neither of us had much money saved, let alone enough money to spend; but we knew we had to come up with a plan to get the money to go. Since Chris was the mathematical one, he wrote up a budget. We figured out our car expenses, how much gas we would need, how to budget for food, and what to do about accommodations. We factored in road tolls, emergency repairs and the cost of the fair itself.

As we began to gather our funds, maps and an itinerary, we investigated renting a small RV so we could save on hotels along the way. We visited an RV rental place off Highway 36 and stopped in to take a look. Most of the units were huge—enough for a large circus family of 15. We found a rather inexpensive camper that had one twin bed and a fold out twin cot. This one had two small side windows, a tiny square kitchen table, a single burner stove, a Barbie doll-sized sink and an overhead skylight dome for lighting. The bathroom was a tiny version of an outhouse. It did have a five-gallon water tank, but lacked the dirt floor covered in pine needles. "Let's check out the beds," I said.

Chris climbed up the small two-step ladder onto the mattress that extended out over the roof of the vehicle. Unfortunately, with his 6-foot 2-inch frame, the tiny space had his legs bent like a crowbar and his arms twisted like a pretzel. That wasn't going to work. We decided that I would take the upper berth and he would sleep on the fold-out cot. Chris turned the small latch and pulled out the cot that was tucked up under the kitchen table. The cot was no better. We surmised that this RV was meant to house only little people. He pushed it back into its hiding place and re-locked the latch. "There's always the floor," he said. After checking a few more units and getting the rental prices, we decided to make the best of the mini one and signed the rental agreement.

The fair opened on Saturday, May 1, 1982. We decided it was best to wait a week before going to make sure all the kinks were worked out logistically and everything was up and running. Chris and I went to see the movie *ET: The Extra Terrestrial* that following Saturday night, and left for Tennessee early on Sunday.

The 15-hour trip down to Knoxville was mostly interstate driving on I-95, I-66, then I-81 through Virginia. We stopped for the night in Roanoke at a small RV park, where we hooked up to an electric outlet for electricity. We heated up bowls of beef stew on our tiny stove and took showers in the life-sized facilities on the lot. All for a mere $5. We took turns sleeping on the cot and mattress; but for Chris, putting down a blow-up mattress on the floor proved to be much more comfortable for him. My small Sony Walkman came in handy for providing white noise for me to sleep, since I didn't have my small desk fan like I did at home.

We made it all the way to the town of Chilhowee, just east of Knoxville, when the rains came. It was about 6 pm when the traffic slowed to a crawl on I-40. The rain was relentless. We decided to pull off onto a side road and wait out the downpour when a small tragedy occurred. The flimsy skylight started to leak, and the next thing we knew we were ankle deep in cold, brown Tennessee water.

I drove the RV down Ashville Highway looking for a place to stay the night and also to get dinner. There was no using the kitchen at this point. I passed a sign for a small motel located about 50 yards ahead. It was simply called Mom's Place, and it had a tiny neon sign that proclaimed vacancy. I pulled the RV into their parking lot. From the looks of it, it was nearly filled. Luckily, the last of the six parking spots was up on a slight embankment, which was perfect.

Once I parked the RV, the nose was up a good 30 degrees from the rest of the vehicle. I put on my raincoat and went around to the back and opened the door. The water started flowing out onto the pavement. I tied a piece of rope from the door to the side railing and opened the door just enough for the water to escape, but not enough that someone could get inside—without cutting the rope, that is. Chris, now adorned with his rain gear, stepped around back as I

was finishing up the security detail. We proceeded to walk up the wet and slippery wooden steps leading to the office at Mom's Place. It was just getting dark as we rang the bell alongside the outer screen door. The swinging shingle above the door was squeaking loudly as if it hadn't been oiled in years, and the side porch light was covered in cobwebs sweetly adorned with wet dew from the raindrops.

After 20 seconds or so, the inner door opened, and a small black woman appeared. She was a frail older lady, hunched over a bit and wearing an old beat-up tattered paisley apron. Her hair, a twirl of tightly woven grey cornrows, peeked out from under what looked like an old Englishman's nightcap. She held onto the inner knob of the screen door and asked if she could help us. "If you would, ma'am, we're in need of a room for the night," we said in unison. "We saw your vacancy sign a little way up the road and were hoping—" She stopped me in mid-sentence and undid the latch holding the screen door. She pushed open the door just enough to get a good look at us. She eyed us up and down a couple of times, trying to get a better view with the tiny amount of light shining from the fixture above.

"Well, this sho' is an awful night to be out tryin' to scrounge up a place to bed up," she said in her very twangy Tennessean accent. "I does have a room," she went on. "But there is one small problem." With that, she inched closer to me. Her deep, black eyes met mine with a profound sense of urgency. She covered her right ear with her hand and spoke directly into my left ear. "Y'all goin' to have to sleep witch yo' manfriend. I only gots one room and it only gots one bed." She didn't think Chris heard her, but he did and let out a small snicker of delight. "I think we can handle that," I assured her we were comfortable sharing tight living quarters. "That'll be 20 bucks up front," she said. "Dinner is extra iffin' you want it."

She opened the door all the way and we stepped into the front foyer. I quickly took out a $20 bill and handed it to her. "How much is dinner?" I asked. "That'll be $2.50 each," she said. I paid her the additional money and she handed me a key. "Yo' room is at the end of the hall. Try to keep quiet iffin' you kin." "They other folks be restin'," she went on. "I'll send yo' dinner in a half an hour."

Sure enough, the room had one twin bed. Luckily, it was long enough to accommodate Chris's long legs, and it had a headboard and footboard. We surmised it was sturdy enough to hold the two of us. The tiny room was sparsely furnished with only a small desk and chair, a simple three-drawer dresser and a tiny folding chair in the corner. The single window overlooked the parking lot, where I could get a good view of the camper. The rain hadn't let up at all, and there were torrents of water running from the parking lot into the street. I grabbed a towel off the bed and began drying myself off. "It could be worse," Chris said. "We could be sleeping in our soppy damp motorhome."

"Yep," I added. "Chilhowee is now our home away from home." Moments later there was a knock at the door. I answered it, and a little boy about ten years old handed me two paper bags. "Here's your dinner, mister. I hope you enjoy it." He turned and walked away, and I closed the door. Inside the bag were two take-out boxes from Lena's World Famous Chitlins of East Knoxville. We both looked at each other, mouths dropping. I had never heard of them before. Chris had, but he had never eaten them. They certainly smelled good; but then again, anything battered and deep fried always smells good.

I opened my box and surveyed the contents. Next to the chitlins were some seasoned french fries, a small container of coleslaw, some packets of apple cider vinegar and hot sauce. I was starving, so rather than ask what they were, I grabbed one and popped it into my mouth. It certainly was different, but no different than the tripe that my father made me eat when we were kids. Tripe is cow's stomach, boiled and covered with marinara sauce and served with spaghetti. Chitlins (I found out later) were similar, but from a pig. They tasted much better drowned in vinegar and hot sauce. After our sparse dinner and some bottled water, we bedded down for the night.

The next morning, the sun came out and it was a clear, beautiful day. We took turns getting dressed and using the facilities, then made our way outside. I climbed up on the roof of the RV and made some simple repairs using—what else—duct tape. I never leave home without it.

We cleaned up the dirty mess and got on the road again. It was a quick 45 minutes to Knoxville, and we got there just after the opening. The fair was fun. There was a lot to see in the two days we spent there, but we both enjoyed the Australian and Chinese pavilions the most. We got to see and touch a part of the Great Wall of China. Australia showed off the first renditions of giant modern windmills, which eventually became wind turbines. The country of Peru had an actual ancient mummy that was unwrapped right there in the amphitheater for all to see. It turned out to be a small child.

We enjoyed lots of other ethnic foods from many countries. We spent lots of time at the German *biergarten*, where the food was incredible and the imported beer was delicious. We didn't, however, partake in the nightly display of chicken dances that went on in the *Strohaus*. Most of that crowd had probably drunk quite a lot to put on such a rambunctious spectacle.

Hungary displayed what was then the largest ever functional Rubik's Cube. I believe it's still there at the Knoxville Holiday Inn, and still working to this day.

Sadly, the fair showed little in the way of energy conservation or innovation. Ford introduced a prototype fuel cell automobile that never caught on. Although they sold a solar-powered hard hat with a tiny whirly-bird on top, there was little else at the fair that promoted solar energy.

All in all, we had a great time at the Knoxville World's Fair—aside from the RV water disaster, the surprise pig-innards dinner at Mom's Place, and the less-than-ideal sleeping arrangements in the motor home. I even stole a light bulb as a souvenir.

A Great Devilish Adventure

Aside from the boardwalks and amusement parks along the shore in New Jersey, there weren't too many other places where a family could go for entertainment. That was, until someone decided to uproot thousands of trees and fill in hundreds of acres of marshland in the southern part of the state. The Pine Barrens became what is now Six Flags Great Adventure.

One day in early 1973, while working in a hi-fi electronics store as a bench technician, I was called into my boss's office. Henry sat me down and told me he got a call from a company called Hardwicke Industries. They were constructing a theme park called Great Adventure near the Pine Barrens. They needed someone to install CB radios, base stations, antennas and everything necessary for the construction crew to communicate while building the park.

Henry asked me if I would spearhead the install. I jumped at the chance and planned to visit the site to arrange the setup of the necessary equipment. In the early 70s, CB radios were all the rage, and everyone from long-haul truckers to redneck ranchers had one. With the help of the construction crew, we set up twenty CB base stations and outfitted almost every working man with a portable walkie-talkie. In about a month's time, the entire 475 acres was wired and operational. I was paid a good commission and given a lifetime park pass for all my hard work.

The park was slated to open in July of 1974. It was around the third week in October '73 when the work crews became aware of the legend of the Jersey Devil from the local residents. A great many of the construction workers were Latino, and their culture believed very heavily in spirits and the folklore of mythical gods.

The legend of the Jersey Devil was just that—a tale; but once a rumor gets started, it is often very hard to eradicate. The legend goes like this:

Sometime in the early part of the eighteenth century, in a New Jersey forest called Pine Barrens, a woman known as Mother Leeds gave birth to her thirteenth child and cried out, "Oh, let this one be a devil!" The child arrived and looked quite normal; but within minutes it morphed into a creature with a horse-like head and bat-like wings. The eyes glowed red, it yelped menacingly and flew up and out of the chimney, disappearing into the dark woods to spend the centuries accosting anyone unfortunate enough to encounter it. The commonly held story of the Jersey Devil bears no resemblance to any sort of reality; however, even those of a skeptic nature would not dare refute such a tale as being a hoax.

One by one, workers exchanged the tale over cigarettes and lunch breaks. About two days before Halloween, a mass walkout of mostly Latino workers occurred. The men spoke of the fear of working in the Pines and encountering the *diablo*, especially near Halloween. They were scared for themselves and their families. Construction management and supervisors got together and tried to reassure the workers that this was just an old wives' tale, but still they refused to go anywhere near the forest. Eventually, the company hired a crew of armed security personnel, who surrounded the worksite to prevent any unauthorized demons from entering the grounds.

The park opened on time and had tremendous success for over four decades. As more time goes by, the tale gets less and less attention; but for me, it was pretty real because I was indirectly exposed to it. I only used my park pass three or four times before eventually moving to Florida. I still think of that time as one of my greatest adventures.

A Potato Changed a Life

While finishing up my college degree in Saint Petersburg, Florida, I needed to choose an elective class to make up some additional credits. After perusing many different options, I chose American Sign Language. My first class was amazing. I picked up on the concept very quickly, and I found myself very comfortable using my hands and body to convey both simple and complex words and sentences. I might attribute this to being brought up Italian and using my wildly expressive hands to convey my messages.

My teacher noticed my unique ability right off and asked if I would consider changing my major to become an interpreter. As it turns out, there was a great shortage of reliable interpreters in the area. She thought I might want to reverse gears and begin training as one. I did give it some thought, but I was already heavily indebted to my other studies in the business field. After graduation and my move to Colorado, I got an unexpected visit from my 19-year-old niece, Sandy, and her friend Elizabeth. They were driving west to Oregon from New Jersey and had decided to stop in Denver.

While they were visiting, I took them out to an Italian marketplace restaurant for dinner. This was a unique place where multiple cooking stations were set up, and you could walk around selecting various dishes, salads, desserts, veggies, etc. I selected a few different foods, some pasta, roasted potatoes and a spinach salad. When Sandy and Liz got back to the table, we started chatting. I had my mouth full of food when Sandy asked me a question.

Without even realizing it, I started signing to her. Once I swallowed, she asked me what I was doing, so I told her. She obviously had never noticed anyone signing before and asked me to teach her a few words. I looked down at my plate and saw the potatoes, took my index and middle fingers from my right hand, made a fist with my left and tapped on it twice with my two fingers. "This is the sign for potato" I said. She tried it. "What's the sign for eat?" she wanted to know. I signed it using three fingers sitting on my thumb and gesturing to my lips.

For the next good hour, I taught her some simple signs. She picked up on them rather quickly, then repeated them back to me. By the time we left the restaurant, she was so smitten with this new ability to speak that she blurted out in the car how she finally found something she was actually passionate about. She wanted more than anything to become an interpreter. It was almost like I was meant to be there in that time and place to show her a new path in her life.

Once she returned home to New Jersey, she immediately registered at Ocean County Community College and began taking American Sign Language (ASL). After studying for a few years, she got her degree and became an official interpreter. I was amazed that such a small gesture on my part could change the entire trajectory of a person's life. I am so enormously proud of her and what she has accomplished; and it all started by me signing a simple word like potato.

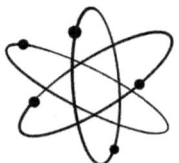

Happiness Isn't Just a Warm Puppy

Everyone's idea of happiness is different. Happiness also depends on your age, your occupation, your social status and even your intellect. Did you often wonder what makes people happy? In America's past, it was said that between 1955 and 1960 more than 40 percent of the population claimed to be extremely happy, the highest in recorded history. Even Walt Disney capitalized on that fact when he opened Disneyland in California in 1956 and proclaimed it to be the "Happiest Place on Earth."

When I was growing up, there were lots of things that made me happy. On occasions, Saturday night was a time when Dad took out the old movie projector. He would set up an irridescent reflective screen in the living room so the family could watch home movies. Thinking back on those evenings, no matter how many times we saw a movie of our siblings celebrating another birthday, one of us falling off our bike and getting bruised, or opening up another unwanted Christmas gift, we never got tired of watching them. It was all happy smiles and wide grins until the projector bulb burned out, which happened a lot. Then it would be back to watching *Gunsmoke* on our tiny black-and-white television.

Mom was her happiest when she got new appliances. Our 12-year-old Kelvinator refrigerator freezer would slowly build up an igloo's worth of ice on all four sides. It eventually reduced the amount of usable space to hold one package of Bird's Eye petite green peas and a Swanson Salisbury Steak TV dinner. My mom's face lit up like a Christmas tree when Dad finally broke down and got us a frost-free model. Mom's happiness was derived from no longer having to chip away at 45 pounds of ice and chasing dozens of tiny chips scattered across the kitchen and dining room.

Even more frightening was that Mom always asked for a new Hoover or Eureka vacuum cleaner for Christmas and her birthday. She said that vacuuming made her happy. She once woke up about half the family when she started vacuuming in the middle of the night. When one of my sleepy-eyed sisters asked her what the heck she was doing, Mom would say that she couldn't sleep knowing that the living room rug hadn't been vacuumed that day.

When I was a kid, going grocery shopping with my mom also made me happy. Once we parked the car in the A&P parking lot, I would grab a grocery cart and push it up to the entrance. Just before the doorway was a rubber entry mat, and when you walked onto it the market doors would fling open to welcome you.

Of course, it wasn't enough to just push the cart along and into the store. I had to drop off the cart inside and go around to the exit side, stomp on the electric magic carpet and watch the doors fling open in the other direction. I was so thrilled by this that I spent the next half hour just stomping on the mat whenever a customer approached to let them go in.

A new pair of Buster Brown shoes made me happy. At the beginning of the school year, all the kids would get a new pair of school shoes. For as long as I could remember, each year Dad would herd all the kids into the station wagon. Away we would go to the Buster Brown shoe store. I was happy getting new shoes, but that picture of the winking kid with his dog, Tige, grinning at me with a hundred sharp pointed fang teeth gave me the creeps. I ripped that decal out of my shoes as soon as I got home.

My school buddy, Bobby Michaels, had a mint 1960 Mickey Mantle outfield baseball card (number 350) that I wanted in the worst way. I tried trading two peanut butter sandwiches, a genuine Stevens gyroscope in its original plastic box, and a fully functional official Boy Scouts multipurpose Swiss army knife, but he wouldn't budge. I pleaded with him at recess and once again on the playground after school, but good ol' Bobby was very stubborn. "This would make me very happy," I said, trying to sound both sincere and convincing.

"Ever since losing my father to the plague, I've been very down," I said, tilting my head downward and trying to muster at least one small tear. "Oh wow, that is really sad," he said. "I can't imagine anything worse than having a dead father," he went on. "So, I guess you can have my Mantle card; but you need to give me at least your pocketknife."

"Gladly," I said. "I'll bring it to school tomorrow."

Bobby put his hand on my shoulder. I lifted my head and said, "Thanks, Bobby."

As I got older and matured, other more important things made me happy. Getting all A's on my report card made me happy. Buying my first car with cash made me exceedingly happy. Moving into and setting up my first apartment made me exceptionally happy. Getting a draft notice didn't. Luckily, I was never called. That made me happy!

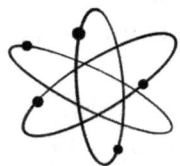

A Slight Distraction

It was an ordinary Saturday morning for the most part, except here I was stuck in the waiting room at my dentist's office. I looked around the room, mentally counting all the people there. A couple of them were noticeably wincing in pain, and a few older men were thumbing through years-old copies of *Field and Stream* magazines with half-torn covers. There was no noticeable background elevator music. A semi-monstrous TV set hung from the ceiling in one corner, facing the room. The sound was muted, but the picture portrayed a person's open mouth showing the destruction of their teeth and gums from years of neglect.

I chose an open seat next to a young boy and sat down. He was your average pre-teen with noticeable signs of acne beginning to show on his slightly oily face, a sure sign that puberty was about to hit him full force at any day. We glanced at each other quickly, and he went back to pushing buttons on some kind of handheld entertainment device. He was either there alone or one of his parents had dragged him along for the ride while they fulfilled their appointment with the dental staff.

I reached over to the table laden with artfully arranged rows of magazines and scanned the titles.

I gently pulled out a copy of *Us*, trying not to upset the symmetry of the queued periodicals, and flipped through the first few pages. Photos of washed-up celebrities dotted the pages, along with various excerpts of disgraces and scandals. After a minute, I flung the magazine back on the table and disrupted one whole row of organized reading material. The kid next to me stopped pushing buttons on his game and looked up at me. "Don't you have a phone, mister?" he asked. I glanced up quickly and noticed, sure enough, everyone else who wasn't reading was tapping and swiping away at their phones.

I turned to him and asked his name. "I'm Jeremy," he said. "What's yours?"

"I'm Lenny," I replied. "Are you waiting to see the dentist?" I asked him. "Nope. My mom is having a

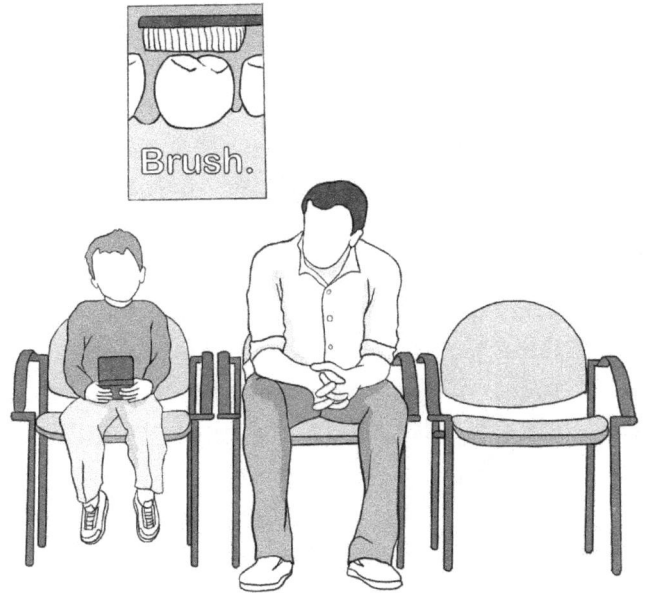

distraction," he replied. I laughed slightly under my breath and attempted to correct him. "I think you mean extraction," I said. He cocked his head to the side and pondered my response. "Oh yeah, that," he said. Then he added, "I don't have a phone yet, but I'm getting one for my thirteenth birthday in three weeks. I can't wait."

Suddenly, our conversation went back to whether or not I possessed a phone. "Well, I do; but I'm not addicted to it like most people," I said. "I don't do Twitter or Instagram, and I couldn't care less who is following me unless I'm walking alone on a dark deserted street in an unfamiliar neighborhood. Then I care."

"My mom talks to Siri all the time," he went on. "She asks her how to make s*auerbraten* and asks her if *General Hospital* will be on at one o'clock today. Once, she wanted to know what time it was in Geneva, where grandma lives."

"When I get my phone, I will never put it down," he said. "I want to know everything," he went on. "I want to be the smartest kid in my class." For a brief moment, I felt sad for Jeremy, but I also felt a bit of jealousy. I wanted to tell him how things were when I was growing up. I wanted to tell him how excited I was to find the answer to a question or problem by going to my set of *World Book* encyclopedias. The 18-book series took up a whole five-foot section on the shelf in the bookcase. Next to them was the *World Atlas*, a thesaurus, a dictionary and the latest edition of the *Farmers World Almanac*. If all else failed, there was the public library, where you could spend hours learning about anything your imagination could dream up.

Somehow, I'd never convince a kid like Jeremy, who, in three weeks, would have the entire world wrapped up in a half-inch thick, five-inch diagonal screen device that he would hold in his hand. I wanted to emphasize that this technology only exists because of the hundreds of thousands of scholars, scientists, historians, inventors, explorers, researchers and professors who toiled endlessly for years to make that little device a reality.

Nowadays, most people are spoiled because they have that instant gratification of getting an answer to anything and everything in a fraction of a second.

The receptionist came into the room holding my chart and announced my name. I got up and said a quick hello to the nurse, then turned around to face Jeremy. "Do me a favor, Jeremy," I said. "First thing you should do when you get your new phone is to look up the word 'extraction.' That will be the beginning of your quest to be the smartest kid in your class."

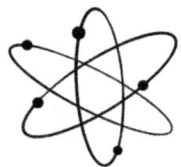

The Incident

When it came time for one of my older siblings to teach me how to drive, it seemed like they always had something else to do that was much more important than me. My oldest sister was late for work. My second-oldest sister had just put curlers in her hair and would never be seen in public, no matter what the emergency. My third-oldest sister owned a Volkswagen bug. It was a 4-speed manual transmission, and she made it clear to me that I would never be able to master that, so I shouldn't try. After begging her for a good hour, she finally agreed and put me in the driver's seat. I was so excited that I nearly forgot to put on pants.

"Pull up the seat so you can reach the pedals," she barked. "Now adjust the side mirror so you can see both the side of the car and the side of the road. Next, adjust the rear-view mirror so you can see if something is behind you." I spent the next ten minutes stalling out the engine. "You're letting out the clutch too fast. You're giving it too much gas. You're braking when you should be accelerating."

The more she shouted, the more nervous I became. I'm sure the other drivers on the road were thinking that this VW was a toy model car that was wound up too tight. As I tried to master the two pedals, we went sputtering down the street, the car bucking back and forth like an unbroken bronco. After many short driving lessons and a few more grey hairs, I finally conquered the shifting mechanism. I became comfortable having other cars in front and behind me. I also began to notice a lot of unusual road signs, not just the ones that were meant to make me stop, yield or turn right on red.

"Why do these people have a hidden driveway?" I asked. "Isn't anyone supposed to know they live there? What are they hiding it from?" My sister just shook her head and said, "Never mind about that." Further down the street there was another strange one that said, "No Outlet". So, I turned to my sister and asked why there were no outlets on this street. "How are the people supposed to plug in their hair dryers and record players?" She just called me a moron and didn't say another word. I had to add that some signs just were totally stupid. For instance, there was one that said, "Water on Road During Rain." Were they just being funny, or was the sign maker smoking one of those funny cigarettes while working?

After a few more lessons, I finally mastered hills, K-turns, parallel parking and drive-throughs; and I passed the driver's test with slightly less than flying colors.

I, like many teens, had found a new independence: my driver's license. But what I didn't have were my own wheels. Back then, my allowance only went so far. Out of a dollar, 34 cents went to school lunches,

35 cents for records, 11 cents for grooming necessities, and the rest was spent on after-school snacks and school supplies. It would be at least three years before I could afford my own car; and hand-me-down cars in our family were few and far between. I did get to drive the family Chevy station wagon, but that was only for going to school and taking Mom to the grocery store. The good thing about that overly huge and extremely ugly car was that it had an automatic transmission. No more bucking bronco VWs for me.

They say no one ever forgets his first car "incident." I certainly did not. On one of my many "Mother transport days," as I liked to call them, my mother decided to sit in the front seat. She usually sat in the back clutching her fist, biting her fingernails, cursing and cringing under her breath while the poor driver took her here and there. Since she was now positioned front and center in the line of sight of the road, it gave her the opportunity to verbally comment on each and every move I made. "Why are you driving so fast? Why are you driving so close behind that other car? Why didn't you turn when I said to?" You could see how these kinds of distractions could get a driver annoyed.

On this particular day, we were returning from a grocery trip, and the back of the wagon was filled with at least ten full bags of groceries. The rear seats were folded down to make room for all of them. As I came up to a traffic light, Mom screamed, "THAT GUY IS GOING TO RUN THE LIGHT!" Without hesitation, I slammed on the brakes. Just as we got out of the intersection, the bags of groceries started flying forward. Next thing I knew, we were knee deep in cans of vegetables. Oranges and apples filled my lap, and the dashboard was now filled with everything you needed to make a good stew. One of the oranges became lodged under the brake pedal, and as I continued to press down on it, my leg was spritzed with orange juice.

We came to a stop on the side of the road. Although dazed and confused, we were alright. I got out, went around to the back of the car and opened the tail gate to assess the damage. If it weren't for the 10-pound bag of all-purpose flour that had burst, it would have been an easy cleanup. After that day, I just gave Mom money for a taxi. I figured that cab drivers had more patience than I would, since they did this for a living. Most of them would not understand my mother's babbling English anyway.

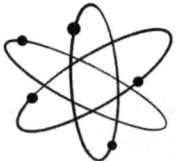

Button Button. Who's Got Yer Button?

Childhood games not only cement solid bonds between friends, but they also teach us that you can laugh at a friend for doing idiotic things and they will still be your friend. Kids love to prank other kids; it's human nature. But when the universe steps in and does something nobody expects, it can seem very funny to some and not so funny to others. Mother Nature played a really nasty prank on poor, unsuspecting Mark and nobody laughed.

It was a sunny Saturday afternoon when eight of our closest friends decided to go to the park and play. Someone suggested Hide and Go Seek, but there were not many trees or buildings in the park that would conceal a kid from the prying eyes of the leader. Baseball was also ruled out because the three ball fields were already occupied by a bunch of older kids from the projects.

Becky suggested a friendly game of Button Button. She just happened to be wearing a rather large, bulky, purple overcoat with one of the 2-inch white buttons barely hanging by a thread. With a good tug, she ripped it off and displayed it to the group. "How do you play it?" asked Mark. "Well," Becky said, "You start off making a circle on the ground, and everyone sits with his or her legs crossed and their palms together. We all start singing the words to Button-Button, and the person who is It slides the button into the palms of one of the kids. They continue to fake giving the button to another kid to throw everyone off. Only one person has the button; but even if you don't have the button, you pretend that you do so the person who has to find it can't tell who has it and who doesn't".

"This is a stupid game," remarked Barry Shingleman. "No, it's a lot of fun. Give it a chance," said Becky. "Okay then, I want to be It," Barry shouted. "Fine!" So, Barry got the button, placed it between his palms and started making his rounds inside the circle. As he circled, he placed his palm inside the palms of each of the seated kids. With a few snide and devilish looks, he continued his rounds. Once he got back to the beginning, he asked "Button button. Who's got the button?" The first kid he started with got to guess. Dennis shouted out, "Mary's got the button". Mary mockingly opened her hand to reveal nothing and stuck her tongue out at Dennis.

The next kid, Sasha, guessed. "Peter's got the button," she said. Peter immediately opened his hand to also reveal nothing. Sasha, being disappointed, hung her tiny head down and sulked for about 12 seconds. Now it was Mark's turn to guess, but he just sat there with his hands folded, his eyes wide open and his mouth gaping. "Well, Mark," Becky chimed in. "What's your guess?" Mark started mumbling something that no one could understand and then pointed down at his leg.

It seemed that he had chosen to sit on an exceptionally large and active ant hill and the little insects were not at all happy about that. They started crawling up his sneaker onto his bare leg and up toward his shorts. Instinctively following each other, the ants formed a nice long trail from the ground up into Marks pants. Luckily, they were not the red kind that everyone knew to stay away from, but the sheer number of them inching their way into Mark's trousers did not please him in the least. Finally, he jumped up and started running around inside the circle of little kids, whacking away the ants with his hand and screaming at the top of his little lungs.

In a matter of minutes, all the kids were swatting the ants from their arms, faces and legs while running into each other with wild abandon. One by one, the little kids fled the park and rushed off to their homes. Most of the mommies and daddies were outside in their yards and gathered up their kids to tend to their panic. I'm sure lots of ice cream was needed to soothe the scared children.

We never found out who had the button that day, and never found it again. It got lost in the shuffle back in the park. The next time we got together to play that game, it was in the safety of one of our family's basements, free from anthills. What we didn't know then was that lots of scary daddy-longlegs spiders live in basements.

BOB: An Inspiration.
A Remembrance of Max

It's been a little over a year since I wrote this book that I lost my best friend Max. They say that time heals all wounds. That may be true for humans, but for me it's taking more than time to get over the loss of my cat. Some days when I wake up in the morning, I expect that Max will be there sitting on the edge of the bed, waiting for me to fully open my eyes and seize the day. I see only the empty blanket. I sink back down into the already flattened pillow and close my eyes, trying to recall the moment. This may sound silly, but I found those moments almost inspirational.

My good friends, Rose and Jim, visited the other night. For my birthday, they gave me a book by James Bowen called *The Little Book of BOB*. I had not heard of this author before, but they knew I loved to read about cats; and the picture of this chubby orange tabby on the cover just stole my heart. I could not put the book down until I was finished. Of course, that is what got me thinking of my beloved Max once again; so here I am writing another short story to honor him.

As anyone who has ever had the good fortune to share his life with a cat can tell you, they are very independent. They're just like humans. We leave our parents' nest to find our own way, to rely on ourselves and to be self-sufficient. We try to make the best out of what life offers. Cats are the same. Max would learn to open cabinet doors to find his own food. If his water dish was empty, he would jump up on the counter and tap his paw on the faucet to let us know.

Max's presence is missed. His inquisitiveness is missed.

I came home from the department store with a do-it-yourself plant stand. I tore into the box and lifted out the pieces of shelf, the Styrofoam packaging and cardboard pieces, and threw them haphazardly around the room. In that moment, I recalled how Max would have heard all the commotion and come running over to see what kind of trouble he could get in with all the new and unfamiliar items that now occupied his domain. He would sniff around the plastic bags, ruffle through the packing, and jump and dive like a kitten, sending packing peanuts flying. Like most felines, he would get bored after about 10 minutes and wander off to find a new adventure.

Bob's book made me appreciate my other cats more. Thankfully, I still had Gus and Samantha, although they were getting up there in age. A good deal of their day was spent eating, sleeping and pooping.

As if he knew the loss of Max made me sad at times, Gus learned to somehow take his place on different occasions. Gus was never a lap cat, but he suddenly became one. Whenever he saw me stretch out on the couch with a book, he would immediately come over and perch himself up on my chest. If he knew I was about to take an afternoon nap, he would inch himself over to me and wait until I settled down to jump up on me and settle himself in.

As I mentioned in my previous story about Max, he loved to chase the laser light. It was one of his favorite things to do. As he got older and weaker, I decided it was best not to tire him with it anymore, so I stashed it away in the junk drawer. The other day, I was rummaging for something and came across it. I took it out and decided to play with Gus and Sam. Sam just stared at it and walked away. Gus was all over it. He scrunched down, his little butt gyrating back and forth, waiting to pounce on the tiny red dot. I moved the light around the carpet and Gus did his best to attack and kill... for about 5 minutes. Then he sauntered back to his little box and flopped over.

I feel a whole lot better having read that book and realizing I still have those wonderful memories of Max that will never fade away. After immortalizing him for over a year, I can finally take the 35 memorial photo frames of him off the mantle and replace them with just one photo of my three favorite feline friends. Thanks, Bob!

That Red Stuff You Put on Spaghetti

As anyone of mostly Italian upbringing can tell you, you don't mess with staunch Italian traditions. For me, it was always picking a seat at a restaurant with my back against a wall, facing the entrance. This was so you could see anyone walking in with a large guitar-type suitcase. Yes, I know—a little paranoid; but I'm still here to talk about it. In Italy, it is still considered bad luck to sit at the corner of any table, as this meant you were never going to marry. My grandmother once told me to never put your hat on a freshly made bed. I, of course, asked why. She told me it would invite death to the next person who slept there.

As a young boy, I remember eating many dinners at my grandparents' house. With traditional Italian pasta dishes, there were always many loaves of round, flattened Italian bread with holes in the center placed on the table. During the meal, the bread was passed around. Everyone would tear a hunk off and hand it to the next person. I never gave it much thought until I read somewhere that in Italy, bread was considered to be a symbol of life. Also, you never placed a loaf of bread upside down or stuck a knife in it.

And speaking of kitchens, I remember getting my very first apartment back in the late 1970s. While setting up my kitchen, I remember something my grandma told me. Make sure you hang a kitchen witch where she can watch over you. I do not remember seeing a witch hanging in grandma's kitchen, but I knew I had to find one for mine. Whether or not it was superstition, as long as I had Gertrude (that's what I called her) hanging up there in the corner, my sauce never burned and my pot of boiling water never spilled over.

This brings me to the last of my Italian traditions. This is the still-controversial name of the red stuff you find on pizza and spaghetti. I was brought up calling it sauce; but many others, including members of my own family, wanted to call it gravy. You see, a lot of this stems from our Sunday dinners, where almost invariably a pot of Sunday sauce sat on the stove, cooking for hours. So we called it pasta sauce. As a pretty good cook, I preferred to think of gravy as that brownish stuff you pour over mashed potatoes, turkey and stuffing, or flour biscuits in the morning at breakfast.

The more I researched this dilemma, the more I realized that those who preferred "sauce" were from the really old Italian school, and those who preferred the word "gravy" were more American in their thinking. Either way, I do believe that with the next generation, the gravy-ites will die out and sauce will be adopted as the new standard.

Just don't get me started on pasta vs. macaroni.

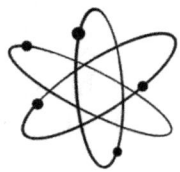

I'm a Travelin' Man

I used to be obsessed with celebrating my birthday day. I still am. When we were kids, my mom would make sure that each kid's birthday was special. We would have a home-made cake with ice cream, the whole candle-blowing-out thing and at least one gift you could count on. As we got older and there were more and more things to celebrate, birthdays became less important. Mom would double up on some just to save time and money. Since both my sister, Nora, and I were born in July (mine on the 10th and hers on the 28th), our combined birthdays would be celebrated at the end of the month. To me, it was not the same. As the years passed, observing my birthday seemed to be less relevant to most of the family, but I still thought I deserved better. After all, I was born a surviving twin. Isn't that reason enough?

Later in life, I realized that if I didn't make any plans for observing my special day, no one else would. Once I grew older, had a decent job and made my own money, I decided to do something special for myself on my birthday. At first, it was buying something frivolous. It would be something I always wanted, but knew I should not be spending my hard-earned money on.

When video games first came out, I saw an ad on

TV for this wonderful game console, the Magnavox Intellivision system. It was priced at $200. For an 18-year-old, that was like a thousand bucks. Once I got it, I realized it was a money pit. I was forever spending money on new cartridges as the games became more sophisticated and challenging. As the technology grew and video games became an American obsession, this overpriced gadget became obsolete and wound up in the attic within a year. I treated myself to years of useless, trivial gizmos that broke too soon and were banished to the garage. At a future yard sale, my discarded toys would eventually spark some 11-year-old's interest and force them to fork over a measly $2 for something I paid over $20 for. From then on, I gave up on buying "stuff".

At the ripe young age of 20, I discovered travel. My first birthday trip was driving across the country from New Jersey to San Bernardino, California. I stopped at some interesting places on the way; but since I was with a group, I couldn't just stop wherever I wanted and really explore. Once I got to the west coast, I got a job, stayed with friends, went to college and began exploring my world.

California in the 1960s was, to say the least, thrilling and exciting for a young person. There were large cities, beautiful beaches, mountains, deserts and everything in between. On my days off, I took short trips to explore those places. The more I traveled, the more I wanted to see. One spring break, I traveled up to San Francisco, driving across the Golden Gate bridge and over into Sausalito. Peering over the bay from Golden

Gate Park was a turning point for me. I just knew I had to see more of the wonderous beauty of the United States—and from there, the world.

I made traveling a quest. Once I saved enough money, I would plan a birthday trip. One year, it would be to a part of the US I had never been to; and the next year, it would be somewhere in Europe. My birthday trips have never disappointed me. I traveled all over the state of Michigan one year, stopping in 20 different cities and towns that covered both the main state and upper peninsula. You don't realize the immense diversity of the people and the land until you've physically been there. I got to see and hear the story of Henry Ford (one of my childhood heroes) in Detroit. I picked delicious cherries on the Traverse City peninsula. I took a boat through the Soo locks in Sault St. Marie and spent my birthday having lunch at the incredible Grand Hotel on Mackinac Island—and all of this was just in the state of Michigan!

My first birthday trip abroad was to Italy. I landed in Rome, traveling as far south as Naples, then to Pisa, Venice, Genoa and many places in between. On my actual birthday, I spent it climbing the 551 steps to the top of St. Peter's Basilica in Vatican City. Climbing to the top of the world's tallest dome at 448 feet truly made for a memorable birthday.

One birthday trip took me to the state of North Carolina, where I tried my hand at zip lining. It was a blast! I toured the incredible Biltmore estate (the largest home in America) and drove through the great Smokey Mountains, one of the most scenic roads in the US. My birthday dinner was at the famous Daniel Boone's restaurant in—where else—Boone, North Carolina. I got to taste good ol' stick-to-the-ribs southern fried chicken served family style in one of the town's oldest buildings. The food was amazing. Instead of birthday cake, they gave me a free dish of spoon bread, a first for me. It's a cornmeal-based cake softened with milk and honey and served with a caramel sauce on top. To be honest, I would have preferred a slice of chocolate cake.

Another of my more memorable birthday trips was to England, Scotland and Ireland. I started out in London, seeking out the usual tourist spots like Tower Bridge, Hyde Park and Buckingham Palace. The best thing in England, though, wasn't shopping at the world's largest store, Harrods. It was sitting in a pub in Earl's Court enjoying a birthday dinner that consisted of steak and kidney pie, a pint of fresh Killian's red beer, and listening to a group of older guys at the bar discussing their daily lives among each other. After about an hour, I felt like I was one of the locals. I also spent some time walking the halls of Oxford University. What a great place to spend your college years if you could afford it.

Traveling north to Scotland, I visited an obscure little science museum in Glasgow. They had the most thorough collection of old telephones, radios and televisions I have ever seen. That was exciting to me. I visited Sterling Castle, built in the 1400s, and dipped my toe in the waters of Loch Lomond.

Once I got to Ireland, I enjoyed walking the cobbled streets in Dublin, Cork and Limerick but what I enjoyed the most was standing on the dramatic 702-foot-high rock formation at the Cliffs of Moher. These rocky cliffs extend a good five miles over the Atlantic Ocean, surrounding the western coastline of Ireland.

Of course, no trip to the Emerald Isle is complete unless you partake in the kissing of the Blarney Stone. It was a complete rip-off, but I can now say I did it.

My birthday night was spent at the Merry Ploughboy's Pub in Dublin. The 200-year-old place offered authentic Irish folk dancing, music and a traditional dinner consisting of Angus Irish Beef cooked in—what else—Guinness beer. In lieu of some ordinary yellow or chocolate birthday cake, I was served a warm Irish Bramley mini apple pie with something they called cream anglaise poured over the top.

On my 50th birthday, I decided to be extra daring. I booked a trip to Hawaii and did three amazing things I probably will never do again in this lifetime. The first was tame compared to the rest. I went snorkeling for the first time in the waters surrounding the island of Molokini, off the coast of Maui. I was treated to an upfront and close look at the most beautiful coral formations, the largest sea turtles and the clearest aquamarine waters. The second thing I did was more adventurous.

Around 4:00 am, I met a tour operator at my hotel on Maui. He drove our group to the top of Mount Haleakala. We watched the most beautiful sunrise from the top of the mountain, then dressed in wet suits, climbed aboard a bicycle and biked down the mountain as the sun came up behind us. The thrill of biking and the views while descending the mountain were too beautiful to describe. At the bottom, we were treated to a wonderful breakfast of fresh hot Kona coffee, Linguica sausages (Portuguese) scrambled eggs and rice—a typical Hawaiian breakfast.

The highlight of my birthday trip was jumping out of an airplane over Oahu. I arrived at a place called the Drop Zone at Dillingham Airfield on the north shore of the island and met the flight people who prep you for what is to come. You could choose how high up you wanted to go to make the fall longer. I chose 12,000 feet, but when I told them it was my birthday, they bumped me up to 14,000 for free. Oh, boy. An additional 12 seconds of free-fall.

After learning how to fall, how to land and what the perils were, I was ready for my tandem jump. To say I was scared to death is an understatement. I was petrified. The skies were clear. There were a few spotty clouds here and there; but according to them, it was a perfect day for a dive. I suited up, put on my goggles and stepped into the Cessna 182 airplane. I was one of four, and I was the second to jump. As we reached the highest altitude, we were motioned to move to the open doorway. The wind was whipping through the cabin while I connected my safety hook to the guy-wire above me. My flying guy (Bryan) gave me the thumbs-up signal, and together we tumbled out of the open door into the vast blue expanse below. My heart was racing a mile a minute. The first thing I felt was my face pulling apart from the force of the wind. About a minute in, I became more confident as Bryan kept patting my head giving me the "all is okay" signal.

As we descended, I became more relaxed and started to really enjoy the ride. We reached the maximum descent speed of 120 miles per hour when something very unusual happened. A rather large cloud decided to get in our way. Since they didn't mention that in the briefing, I was a little concerned. Bryan again tapped me on my helmet assuring me that it was nothing to worry about. Within a minute, the nice blue sky had turned to misty grey, and both my goggles and my jumpsuit were soaked. I didn't mind being wet, but the raindrops hitting my face with hurricane force were quite painful.

You see, when you are down on the earth, the raindrops hit you with a rounded bottom, so they're quite gentle. When you fall into them from the top, their little pointed ends are like porcupine needles, and they sting. Luckily, we passed through that cloud quickly and it was clear blue skies once again. We landed without incident. Bryan told me that I was extremely fortunate to experience a rain cloud fall, that it was quite rare. People perform multiple jumps so that it may someday happen to them. I guess I got a happy birthday soaking for the first time in my life.

On many other birthdays, I spent them traveling, and I have never been disappointed at all. Everywhere I've gone, there have been amazing things to see and learn. From rainforests in New Zealand to mountainous rail journeys in Norway, historic places of interest like the Louvre in Paris, or the remains of the wall in Berlin, the frozen Yukon in Alaska, the steamy bayous of Louisiana, the Martian surface of Iceland, walking along the freedom trail in Boston, climbing the Sydney Harbor bridge at night, riding a Jeep through Joshua Tree National Park, and taking in a live Broadway show in NYC, there is so much to experience and enjoy.

Most of my family have never been outside of the US, and some not even too far from their home states. I am so glad I've had the time and the resources to see a good part of this world. There is still much more of it I hope to see, as long as I have the means and my good health. As the old saying goes, "It's not so much the destination as it is the journey".

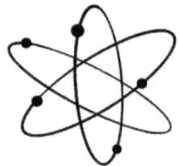

My Ban-Lon Phase

Some humans are gullible and easily influenced into buying into the latest craze or fad. Growing up, I did not usually follow the ever-changing fads in fashion, but I still wanted to blend in with the "in" crowd. Back in the late '60s I saw an ad on TV for Ban-Lon shirts for men. There was this svelte guy sitting at a café and sporting a well pressed pair of Chinos, argyle socks, penny loafers, and sipping on what looked like a mid-day mimosa. He was facing the camera. His dark, wavy hair was messily combed back, and a small curl hung down onto his forehead, no doubt trying to resemble the Man of Steel. He had the whitest teeth, and by his posture you could tell he was fairly confident about who he was and where he stood in society. But what I remembered most about the commercial was his shirt. He was wearing a nicely fitted Ban-Lon knit shirt in sage green. The shirt had not one single wrinkle in it. The three small white buttons coming down from the neck did not distract from you noticing his youthful gym-sculptured torso and abs. The more I watched, the more I was convinced I could pull off that same look, except for the hair curl and some slightly yellowish front teeth. Back then, I had a 30" waist that I would die for to have again. Even though I did not possess six-pack abs, I was working on improving at least two of them.

Ban-Lon made at least 100 different styles of pull-over shirts, some with crazy designs, some in V-neck and crew styles, and some with front side pockets with an additional little white button covering the opening. If a guy had the great fortune to have that perfect body type to show off in a tight-fitting garment, I cannot imagine him wanting to mess up that image by shoving a pack of Marlboro cigarettes into his shirt pocket. It would just throw off his entire preppy look.

The first chance I got, I stopped into the W.T. Grant store and made a bee line to the men's department. I passed by the large assortment of elephant bell bottoms, Nehru jackets, leather chain belts, and finally saw a selection of Ban-Lon shirts. I was already set on buying the sage green; but when I saw the variety of colors for sale, I could not decide on just one. I opened each one, placed it up against my chest and stood in front of the display mir-

ror admiring all the rich bright colors. I bought six.

Luckily, I wasn't caught up in that whole tie-dye revolution of my time, either. People dyed just about everything they owned: shirts, pants, bedsheets and underwear. I'm sure I wouldn't be caught dead going to an anti-war rally in some major city wearing my dull boring Ban-Lon shirt, even if it was accompanied by a pair of very heavy, bulky-looking corduroys with a chain link belt.

Like many of my peers, I also succumbed to buying at least one polyester leisure suit in my past. Looking back at some old photos, I said what many other guys probably said at that moment. "What was I thinking"? I must blame that impulse on Mr. John Travolta. When he donned those three-piece skintight suits and danced up a storm in *Saturday Night Fever*, the nation was hooked. I wish I could have avoided that trend.

Introduced to America in the late '60s by those radical, hippie-types across the pond, the leisure suit became the go-to apparel for both the anti-establishment groups and the "now" generation of disco followers.

Fortunately, that fad (like many others) only lasted a short time. The man's one-piece nightie also did not catch on. Like me, many other guys preferred to sleep either *au naturel* or with just boxers and a T-shirt. I'm sure Sears lost a small fortune on that investment.

In the late '70s it seemed like a lot of men's clothing was made with knitted wool. Mannequins were dressed in either knitted ponchos and tunics, or skintight bright colored satin yoga pants. Let's face it, you had to be in pretty good shape to pull off a pair of those tights with a loud obnoxious multi-patterned Hawaiian shirt. And most of the shirts would be cut very low so you could show off your gym body to the world, if you had one.

I had the unfortunate fate of receiving a dark blue, knitted belt sweater one Christmas from who I thought was my very cool godmother. It was sleeveless with eight buttons down the front and reached down to the middle of my thigh. The belt was also knitted and was adorned with this seriously ugly belt buckle right in the center, just below my waist. You know that thing went immediately to the thrift shop after the holidays.

For reasons unknown, the more men's clothing looked like bad living room wallpaper the more popular they became. Perhaps it was because so many people were experimenting with LSD and other new recreational drugs. They just didn't realize they looked like pimps or hustlers. I guess we all wanted to belong, so we followed the masses. I, too, sported a pair of 4" high shoes. To be honest, they were extremely uncomfortable, and after a few hours of strutting myself on the dance floor of the local disco, my feet were ready to fall off. I eventually donated them to charity.

As with many popular fads, the polyester and satin revolution finally came to an end in the middle '80s, and it was back to the usual cotton and nylon blends. Denim jeans and jackets replaced ponchos and tunics, and some fashion designer somewhere decided that skintight short-shorts and cropped top T-shirts on men would catch on. Men somehow thought that wearing 5" to 7" skimpy shorts were sexy, and that showing bare thighs would somehow attract an abundance of sexual suitors. Truth is, they were extremely uncomfortable, crotch-wise. I remember trying on my first pair of Ocean Pacific light blue corduroy cut-offs. Sure, they looked good when I still had my petite 30" waist, and they were very forgiving when I tried my hand at rollerblading; but again, they were not particularly comfortable. Let's just say that I did not want to begin speaking in a tenor voice, so I gave them up. Enter Mr. Tom Selleck, Sean Connery and Mr. Don Johnson. Between *Magnum P.I., Hawaii Five-O* and the Bond movies, men's clothing took on a whole other dimension. Now it was loud print Hawaiian shirts and snow-white pant & jacket ensembles. With just a white T-shirt underneath and shorter shorts, it left nothing to the imagination.

Rock bands from the '80s began wearing cut-offs, leather jackets without shirts, chains and vests. Aside from the wild hair, those guys who sported manly hairy chests did not hesitate to show them off. I'm glad I didn't waste my hard-earned money on a lot of the fashion crazes from those days. I did not want to be like Jon Bon Jovi or David Lee Roth, and I couldn't really pull off the Prince purple look. I opted for the clean-cut look of Tom Cruise and Rob Lowe, and that suited me just fine. My Ban-Lon shirts eventually wore out and faded with time, and I replaced them with other shirts that proudly showed off my incredible 2-pack abs.

The Bargain Basement

One of my mother's favorite stores was John's Bargain Store. There were multiple outlets all over New Jersey, and mom had a detailed map of all of them stuck to the refrigerator with an Esso Tiger Tail magnet. Because of our unusually large family, the word "bargain" never escaped her vision—not on TV or in the weekly circulars that would pile up in our mailbox three times a week. Mom knew how to squeeze a dime to make it a quarter just by studying the ads and making critical purchases. She was a whiz at recycling before it even became a thing. A pair of long winter pants that had one too many holes became a pair of shorts, hemmed just right and put in a storage bin marked "summer stuff."

Used tea bags and coffee grounds became either dye for changing dingy, used-to-be white T-shirts into brown ones for gym class; or it became fertilizer for our summer vegetable garden. Those old shoes that no longer fit my older sister got handed down to the next in line, modified with cut-out cardboard inserts for them to grow into. Mom always said it was not because we were poor; on the contrary, it was being economical. Sure, tell that to the kid who wore someone else's prom dress and was called out by their peers who remembered it from last years prom. After a few unintentional falls, getting accidentally stepped on, and even a revenge-driven arm decapitation, my youngest sister received an almost indestructible soft, cushiony Raggedy "Nelly" doll that Mom had fashioned from a pair of Dad's old long johns and three months' worth of dryer lint.

Mom always taught us kids the value of a dollar. Most of us who grew up working a few menial jobs, making far less than minimum wage, knew just how hard it was to make those dollars stretch.

Today, I still practice what she taught me. I still look for bargains! When I go grocery shopping, I head over to what I call the bargain basement section of that department. I know exactly where the day-old baked goods are, and I make that one of my first stops while shopping. If I happen to see a bunch of others flitting around, I will sneakily squeeze myself in and start moving around the various bags and packages looking for just the right item. My mind will be racing with thoughts of making perhaps a small meatloaf with a loaf of day-old artesian bread. Maybe I could make a nice tiramisu dessert using that expired package of lady fingers that would have cost me at least three times as much if they were fresh.

By the way, once you put slightly stale lady fingers in with vanilla pudding and mascarpone cheese, they get soft. Nobody would even know you got them from the bargain basement bakery. I also try to nab that bag of day-old French rolls. Once you put garlic oil and spices on them and toast them, you wouldn't even know they were slightly stale to begin with. As with any rack of bargain items, there will always be something there to tempt you. Even though you know you wouldn't spend the money on them, you try to convince yourself that it's STILL A BARGAIN. This is how they can get you to fork over five dollars for a box of a dozen, slightly insipid, chocolate glazed cake donuts. Just a note here: don't go to the bargain basement bakery department when you are hungry. You will succumb to the delightful vision of those twelve fancily decorated donuts sitting there all alone, and you will salivate slightly while adding them to your cart.

As in most grocery stores, there will always be some sort of mark-down shelf. Here is where you really need to have your wits about you. You will probably find 35 cans of last Halloween's pumpkin spice cookie frosting that nobody wanted in the first place. They will be marked down to an incredible 25 cents, and your mind will be scrambling to find a rational excuse for buying all 35 of them. *Hmm*, you think. *Will they stay good til next October?* Uh oh, you spotted that familiar small jar of Nonesuch mincemeat pie mix. Now you think, *have I ever made a mincemeat pie in my life?* Well, no; but there is always a first time isn't there? You pick it up and look at the expiration date. It's seven years old and still here in the bargain basement section of the unwanted goods. I guess I will pass on that one.

Next, I saw a bunch of spice jars all stacked in a row. I started picking them up to see if there were any worth buying. Spices generally have a short shelf life, but some can last years if they are sealed. I lifted up the first one: mustard powder. Nope. Will never use that. Lavender. Now, what the heck would you even use lavender in, anyway? Next: alum. Not sure what that is used in, but it's probably not too popular if it's in this collection. Pass.

I finally stumble on something worthwhile. A small vial of anise extract. Now, for those of you who aren't Italian, you would just pass that up also; but this is one of those rare flavorings that you must have if you're making Italian Christmas cookies. It's marked down to a quarter. I scrambled through the rest of the bottles, hoping to find a few more. Sure enough, there were three. This find alone was worth the trip. Before leaving, I rummaged through a mixed bin of odds and ends just for the heck of it. There were a couple of pink binkies, a jar of Metamucil, a smashed up taped package of Mothers Dutch almond cookies, two boxes of Jiffy corn muffin mix, a pair of cheap Chinese tweezers, and a couple of bags of stale Campfire brand pink marshmallows. Okay, on to the meat department.

The expired meat department is where you have to be really careful. If you're like me and have a spare freezer, it's worth finding a couple of packages of day-old ground beef or a few rib-eye steaks. Prices for a decent steak today are through the roof, so finding a decent bargain here is worth gold. As I mentioned, if you have the room in the freezer or a spare one, you can always freeze the meats for later. Check for freshness and quality.

It helps if you are the only one digging around in the bargain meat department. An unsuspecting shopper may grab that top sirloin roast right out of your hand if you're not careful. I once tussled with a woman over a package of brats. I would have won if I had three-inch fingernails like hers.

So, thanks to my mom, I cut coupons, look for sales and shop around for the best price on most things. When I find those fantastic bargain basement items while on my shopping trips, it makes the whole journey worthwhile.

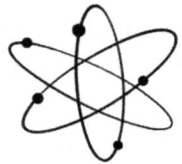

Oh, No! Not Another Collection!

Kids were like a gold mine to toy and cereal companies. On any particular Saturday morning, these companies would bombard your 9" inch black-and-white television screen with advertisements for everything from bubblegum to insect-making rubber toys, to goldfish and turtle aquariums.

If you were lucky to have parents who owned a small diamond mine in North Africa, you could probably ask for any toy you saw. It could be delivered by plane right to your front door in a week. We weren't so lucky. Being from a large family, we didn't always get everything we whined or cried for, so it was difficult for companies like Mattel to convince my parents that I absolutely couldn't do without the latest "thing maker".

If I even mentioned that all my friends had a particular toy, Mom would just tell me to go over to their house and play with theirs.

My friend, Peter, got his very first kiddy record player for his 6th birthday. He invited a bunch of us kids over for his party and couldn't wait to try it out. I was very jealous. After the cake and ice cream, we went up to his bedroom. He tore into his new Mickey Mouse phonograph. It came with a bunch of Peter

Pan "indestructible" vinyl yellow records. I'm not sure what they meant by indestructible, but if you put them in the hands of 7-year-old Jeremy and 6-year-old Alicia, you could find them flying through the air aimed at the nearest desk lamp or stuffed giraffe. Upon missing those targets, the wall would definitely stop the flying records. They would wind up in a heap of pieces next to the dresser. Peter didn't get upset, because his parents would just go out and buy more. He enjoyed throwing them as much as anyone.

On many occasions, we would have to take snacks to school. Sometimes we would go on day trips to the local park or zoo, and other times we would just have a field day where we hunted for bugs or dead reptiles in the fields behind the school. These afternoon trips always included a rest period, and the teacher would sit us down at a picnic table where we would have our snacks. I remember opening my snack bag to find one of my favorites—Wise brand potato sticks. These toothpick sized potato sticks were so delicious and addictive. You could eat that entire bag and perhaps two or three more, and they only cost a quarter. Years later, I learned a secret that the sticks were dipped in sugar and deep fried. Just another way for companies to hook you.

On many hectic weekends, mom was always too busy to make us oatmeal or Cream of Wheat cereal. Instead, she would sit us down at the table and place a large package of Kellogg's 18-pack mini box cereal assortment in front of us. To us kids, this was just like winning the lottery. There was an assortment of Froot

Loops, Rice Krispies, Cocoa Krispies, Frosted Flakes, Corn Pops and our least favorite, Corn Flakes. These little boxes were pure genius from a company standpoint. You would take a small knife and make a cut through the cardboard right down the center. Then two more slices across the top and bottom of the box. You then opened up the box like cellar doors. Next, you sliced through the thin wax paper inner bag and poured milk right into the box. After eating, you just tossed the box in the trash and there was NO cleanup. Other cereal companies soon got on the bandwagon and came out with their own mini variety box packages.

Out of all the toys we had as kids, aside from my model trains, I used to spend hours with my Waterful ring toss. This toy was a plastic water tank with a dozen or so small colored rings suspended in the water. There were a few plastic pegs sticking up, and you had to push a button on the front where a lever would push the rings up into the water. Hopefully, they would land and stack up on the pegs like bean bag toss or horseshoes. If you got all the red ones, you scored more points. If you took a photo of your success and sent it to the company, they would send you back a special decoder ring sized especially for you. You could then show it off to all your jealous friends.

I collected popsicle wrappers like most kids did in our neighborhood. Fudgesicles and flavored ice pops came in thin waxy wrappers with a picture of Popsicle Pete on the front. Just above his photo was written, *Save these bags for SWELL gifts*. Everything

was SWELL growing up. If things went the way you wanted them to, that was SWELL. If your friends commented on your new bike, it was SWELL. In today's offbeat language, it would either be COOL or DOPE.

Anyway, you had to send away for the catalog which listed all the swell gifts you could get with 50, 100 or even 200 wrappers. That was a lot of frozen snacks you had to consume just to get a Joe Balooka blow-up punching bag. It made us kids resort to rummaging through many smelly and filthy garbage cans in the neighborhood just to collect our quota. This was another example of how these companies preyed on kids to get them to buy more products.

With all the talk on TV and radio about the Soviet Union and A-bombs, aliens and space invaders, companies took advantage of our naive little minds and tried to sell us anything and everything ATOMIC. A macaroni company, Buitoni, came out with pasta in the shape of space men. Wouldn't you know, each box came with a free, different and exciting toy in every box. On the front of the box was a huge graphic of a rocket ship racing into outer space with the earth behind it. This, of course, had nothing to do with nutritious protein or enriched pasta, but everything to do with buying all six packages to amass your exciting collection of plastic planets.

Not to miss a beat, the Brach's candy company came out with a "rocket mix" of sweet, gooey candies with a two-inch plastic space man included inside every box—a must for every kid trying to build his own interplanetary space station. Kellogg's re-invented something called PEP, the solar cereal which was just the usual whole wheat flakes. This time, it was endorsed by Superman and Tom Corbett, space cadet, as seen on TV. Of course, there were four different boxes to choose from, each with more intense space related graphics printed on them.

One enterprising company called TNT Popcorn came out with a plastic USA Gemini space capsule containing one and a half pounds of yellow Jet Pop popcorn, and it sold for an amazing 36 cents. I'm sure that container is worth a fortune today.

A few decent companies were not just only about rotting our young teeth. They actually sold products that did some good. In the 1960's, a company created Crazy Foam, which was just a foamy shaving cream in an aerosol can with funny plastic lids attached. There was an Indian brave, a purple skeleton, a large bug-eyed blue fish, an underwater scuba diver, a one-eyed professor and a large yellow beaked bird. Once again, kids begged moms and dads to purchase all of them so they could have yet another collection.

Another brilliant ad man took the popularity of the *Flintstones* television cartoon and came out with multiple vitamins aimed at kids. Parents brought them like crazy, since the One-A-Day brand they trusted for themselves should be just as good for their children. What kid could refuse to eat the likeness of Dino the dinosaur or Bam-Bam, the prehistoric little caveboy.

One thing I am thankful for is that those companies that preyed on our parents to get us to buy toys and cereal didn't actually break our piggy banks. Many large companies today force us to upgrade to bigger and better cellular phones costing upwards of a thousand dollars just to say, "Now you have the latest and greatest." They bombard us with ads to buy bigger and more expensive cars because our mini 2-door sedan just won't cut it on today's highways. I only know that I did without heated seats for over 50 years and survived. That 19" inch color television that got us through 20 adolescent years is obviously no match for that new 75" or 85" LED theatre-vision monstrosity that takes up an entire wall in our living room.

Okay, just for clarification, my cell phone is over four years old, my 22" flat screen TV is over 10 years old, and both and working fine; and my 2017 4-door sedan has never given me the least little problem. But every now and then, I will still splurge on a two-dollar bag of deep-fried, sugar-laden potato sticks.

150 Miracles

I'm going to go out on a limb here and guess that a lot of you reading this book will attest to tasting at least one variety of bar soap in your life. I can remember two distinctly. One was Dial. With our ultra-large family, we always had a dozen or so bars of Ivory soap in the house. This was the cheapest soap, and it did a great job of sprucing up a bunch of dirty kids after an exhausting day of playing hide-and-seek or Cops and Robbers. But in our family, like a lot of other strict Roman Catholic ones (I'm certain), a bar of Ivory came in handy to wash out the mouth of any little heathen who took the Lord's name in vain or questioned the validity of any of the more than 150 biblical miracles.

Upon returning home from Catechism class one Saturday morning, my mother asked me what I had learned. I started talking about Noah and his ark. As I had listened to Sister Agatha tell about how Noah built a giant ark and assembled two of every single animal in the world on this ship, my logical mind wandered and I got very confused. Like most teachings in the bible, I was told to just accept that they were true and to never question them; but as I got older, I couldn't suppress my inquisitiveness about certain "facts".

So, when mom started questioning me about my

lesson, I immediately blurted out, "How come the lions didn't eat the zebras? Where did they store all the food and water for the millions of creatures that were supposedly on that ship for 40 whole days?" Mom's usually cheerful face suddenly changed, and with a slightly raised voice she told me to just accept that the Lord provided everything for Noah, and he knew exactly what he was doing. Of course, that wasn't a good enough answer for me, so I proceeded to question it some more. "How did he get dingos and wallabies from Australia and penguins from the Arctic? They didn't have trains or airplanes back then."

By this time, my mother refused to answer and just said, "Just as Noah trusted God concerning unseen things, so too should we trust God in the things we cannot witness".

"But—" She put her middle finger up to my now closed mouth. "Not one more word," she said. "But what about the dinosaurs?" Mom stormed out of the living room and returned within minutes with a freshly opened bar of Ivory soap. She grabbed me by my collar bone and shoved the soap into my mouth. I started gagging and choking and finally spit it out all over the carpet. "Not another word, do you hear?"

It would be many years later before I questioned anyone in authority about any of the remaining 149 miracles from the bible.

Discipline

Parents often have different and odd ways of disciplining their kids. Some parents are the loving type who try to inject a little compassion into the lesson along with the punishment. My parents were authoritarian, not authoritative. Well, let me just say, they probably didn't know any better back then; but they tried to do their best.

My older sister had the task of collecting the family laundry from the two hampers in the bathrooms and taking it down to the basement on laundry days. With 11 family members, that old Speed Queen washer hardly ever saw a day off. We kids knew the routine well and were charged with picking up all the dirty clothes around our rooms to make sure they got to their respective hampers in plenty of time for pickup.

One Saturday morning, my sister went snooping around in the boys' bedroom and found a pair of dirty, black-and-blue size 9 argyle socks under the bed. The smelly evidence was handed to the first parent who showed up. The next thing we knew, my two other brothers and I were standing in an interrogation line. Normally, one of us would fess-up and the whole matter would be dropped after receiving a mild sentence. Punishment might be getting no dessert at dinner, window cleaning detail or the dreaded sitting with Grandma while snipping off the ends of green beans for what seemed like forever.

Unlike my other brothers, I liked spending time with my grandmother, even if it included snipping green bean ends. Gram always had an interesting story about growing up in Italy and what it was like living in a small Sicilian village, washing clothes on a rock in the river and baking bread in the communal town square oven with a bunch of her neighbors. I have her to thank for my insatiable appetite for traveling.

My two brothers blamed me for the misplaced argyle socks. After a few minutes of back-and-forth bickering, Dad informed me that since I was the oldest, I should have known better. He would decide the appropriate castigation at a later date. Sometimes, I hated being the oldest.

If you went to Catholic school, you were generally exposed to several discipline techniques. Nuns had truly little compassion for those kids who got out of line. They often walked up and down in the classroom, chatting while casually smacking a 12" wooden ruler into their palms. The classic was having that ruler smacked against your knuckles if you spoke out loud, rough-housed or did not have your homework. Another favorite was pulling you out of the room by your ear. These punishments today would likely result in an irate mother storming into the principal's office; but back then it was just business as usual.

It seemed like mothers could not wait to kick us kids out of the house in the mornings so they could get on with their chores or socialize with friends. They called you in when dinner was ready and let you back out, telling you to come inside when the streetlights came on. Even though we were not supervised every minute, most of the time we knew right from wrong.

I remember playing a friendly game of stickball one day with some neighborhood kids. Suddenly, the ball took a different trajectory and put a hole smack dab in the middle of Mr. Johnson's front bay window. Hearing the sound of broken glass hitting the ground is not something any kid wants to hear while holding the very bat that would incriminate you.

Mr. Johnson was not a happy man as he approached us, his facial expression one of intense rage and looking for vengeance. Our first reaction to run away wouldn't help. Every neighbor knew every kid and every kid's parents.

I am not quite sure what my punishment was that day, but it had to be something along the usual. I do know that I forfeited at least two years' worth of birthday money to pay for that window.

Back in the day, parents hit you because that's how they disciplined you. It may have been just a smack on the head, or literally being put over dad's knee for a spanking. Sometimes, it was getting chased around the house and hit with a belt, a mop or broom handle. Parents who themselves were raised with that kind of discipline tended to continue the pattern. In many homes, a common threat was, "Just wait until your father gets home." Since my dad worked at least three jobs, he hardly ever came home. It was usually Mom or one of my older sisters who had to lay down the law. I still have one nice sized knot in my skull to this day as a result of an airborne frying pan for upsetting my older sister. Honestly, I cannot even remember what I did.

I was never fond of standing in a corner for an hour, either. This seemed to be one of the ways parents found to teach you a lesson. Today it's called a time out. Back then, it was a standard discipline for a misbehaving kid. Mom always picked a corner next to an open window so I could hear my friends and neighbor kids having a good time playing in the yard or street. Knowing I couldn't be a part of that was the worst punishment of all. Mom was a smart cookie!

For the most part, I don't think my family's upbringing did us much harm growing up. No one became a murderer, no one went to jail for embezzlement, and not one of us grew up being an arsonist or drug dealer.

Yes, things have certainly changed in the past 50 or so years. Today, a lot of married people are perfectly fine without having any kids at all, and a lot of them don't even get married; they just live together and raise a child or two.

A lot of kids are raised by a single parent, as well. While working dads and stay at home moms were the norm back in the 1960s, that family dynamic has dramatically changed. Today, there are more stay-at-home dads and more working moms in the field than ever before.

Nowadays, with both parents needing to work to make ends meet, discipline has changed. Growing up, my parents had to worry if their daughters were necking in the back seat of their boyfriend's dad's sedan, or that their son was showing his ill-gotten girlie magazine to his friends behind the bleachers at school. Punishment was taking away the car for a week or restricting television.

Today, parents no longer threaten with, "You will go to your room without supper!" Now, it's taking away your smartphone or tablet and cutting off your Twitter and Instagram accounts.

Personally, I think I learned more valuable lessons from not having my bike to ride for a week than not being able to post a photo of me and my friends eating hot dogs down at the local shake shop.

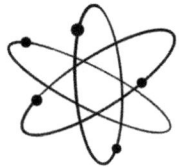

Accident Prone

Humans are a strange bunch. Why is it that we laugh our tails off when we see someone fall down on the ice or crash their bike into a row of garbage bins? We don't think it's that funny when we do some really stupid things and wind up getting hurt. However, as soon as it's over and forgotten about, we can't wait to tell anyone who will listen about our misfortunes. We love to tell the tale of how we got stinking loaded, fell from our bar stool and wound up in a fetal position on the floor. We embellish the story by adding that the surrounding people started laughing up a storm, until someone realized that you had a few facial lacerations and needed immediate medical attention.

Television is notorious for sensationalizing people getting the crap knocked out of them. There are some shows that gain incredible audience viewership because they exploit humans getting beat up, buckets of goop dropped on them from above, being dunked in slime, and the occasional equivalent of getting tarred and feathered on national TV. What a human won't do for a few hundred dollars. This is not a new thing. Ever since the dawn of TV, the more outlandish the prank on an unsuspecting contestant, the more applause they got and the higher the ratings became. One of the first game shows was called *Queen for a Day*. It focused on ordinary housewives who were experiencing some very difficult hardships in their lives. Maybe it was a loved one who was battling cancer, or someone whose home was being foreclosed on by the bank, or a woman whose husband landed in jail for stealing food for his family. Women on the air sobbed loudly and uncontrollably while telling their sad stories, and the one who cried the most got the sympathy of the audience.

If I remember correctly, they actually had an on screen "Clap-O-Meter" that measured the loudness of

applause by which to choose the winner. Once chosen, the winner received a dozen red roses, a crown placed upon her head, a red velvet cape over her shoulders, and was given a new oven, washer & dryer or other prizes donated by the sponsor. Something that was supposed to be inspiring and uplifting was nothing more than a pity party that rewarded the women who had the worst possible luck.

Shows like *The Carol Burnett Show*, *Bewitched* and *The Lucy Show* were highly successful because the main characters fell down flights of stairs, got pies thrown into their faces, were turned into toads, trees or dogs, or fell down into vats of grapes while trying to stomp them into wine. We laughed then and are still laughing today.

The networks will do just about anything to sell another SUV, promote another soft drink or get you to buy one of those busy body, do-all, answer-all, home invasive contraptions like *Alexa*.

On one of those prime time shows dubbed *Game of Games*, contestants are literally and physically thrown across the stage on mechanically operated devices to see who can fall the fastest, get their faces strewn with some of the most vial fluids, stumble and stagger over the strangest of obstacles and overcome even more difficult situations to win a boatload of money. And the audience laughs even harder. I'm guessing humiliation, embarrassment and disgrace are the new values people try to achieve just to make some dough.

Let's face it, we all do stupid things and most of them are by accident; but to put yourself in those situations to risk injuring yourself so Buick can sell another car, or so that your personal device can order tonight's dinner, doesn't sound very smart to me. I prefer to simply put on a pair of ice skates, venture out on some frozen pond somewhere and hope I don't wind up on the 6:00 news. I may be accident prone, but I'm sure I wouldn't want the whole world to know about it, even for two hundred dollars.

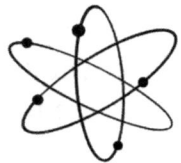

The Thomas Crown Roast Affair

My youngest sister did not have much luck in the dating department. Although she was funny, witty and smart, Maryann did not attract many eligible suiters easily. Her older sisters were always hounding her to get out there, but she was content just doing her own thing.

My nephew Chris's parents were throwing him and his baseball team a party for winning some division championship. They found and rented a hall for the shindig and hired a local mom and pop catering outfit to supply the food and drink. They were expecting about 50 people, so they needed at least 3 servers. The whole family was invited to the party, but Maryann said she was not interested in attending. Of course, like the meddling sisters they were, the other three of them pestered her until she gave in.

On the afternoon of the party, one of the guys who was supposed to serve had to drop out for some unknown reason. The owner called just about everyone he knew to fill in, but on such short notice he could not find anyone. As a last resort, his friend told him that he knew of a body who could possibly stand in. That body turned out to be a guy named Robbie. Rob was a grease monkey by day. He was not very well educated, but he knew his way around a 427 V-8 like nobody's business.

Rob answered the phone and his friend told him of his dilemma. He offered Robbie a chance to make a few extra bucks and mentioned that there would be lots of food. Rob loved to eat. He wasn't so much particular about what he consumed, but more about how spicy, hot, oily, greasy and unhealthy it was.

Robbie spruced himself up. He managed to remove almost all of the grease stains from his arms and face and found a semi-whitish yellow shirt to put on, along with a pair of black Chinos. He hopped onto his Harley and made it to the reception hall with time to spare.

By the time my sisters and I made it to the hall, there were at least 30 or so people there, and the food line was in full swing. Rob was dishing out mashed potatoes and gravy when my sister approached him with her serving tray stretched out in front of her. "You want potatoes, ma'am?" he asked. Their eyes locked. She was a bit smitten by Robbie's azure blue eyes and just nodded her head.

They say that love finds you when you are least expecting it. That was the case with Maryann and Robbie. She managed to get some time to chat with him and she was enamored. It was getting late, so I decided to leave. I told Mare that I was taking off, and she asked Rob to drive her home so they could spend more time together. He agreed and off I went.

They started dating seriously, and after a couple of months, Maryann asked if I would make a special Sunday dinner and invite Rob over. I agreed, and we chatted briefly about the menu. "I really want to impress him," she said, "But you know I can't even make a hamburger without burning it."

"Don't worry," I said. "I'll make it special."

I went to the butcher shop the Friday before the dinner and ordered a beautiful crown roast. In case you don't know what that is, it's a special pork loin rib formed into a circle with the ribs up. It is carefully seasoned with dry herbs and very slowly cooked for up to four hours on very low heat. When cooked just right, the meat falls off the bone and it melts in your mouth. The following day I went by the butcher's market and picked up the roast. It was beautifully trimmed and seasoned, and it even came with seven tiny little white chef's hats to adorn the seven jutting rib bones. I let the roast marinate in the fridge the entire day.

I got up early on Sunday morning and started preparing dinner. I took the roast out of the fridge and let it warm up for a few hours. I covered each rib with aluminum foil and set it on a rack in a shallow pan with a few inches of water. I turned on the oven to 250 degrees and placed the roast on the lower rack. I set the timer to 2 hours for the first checkup. I prepared scalloped potatoes, candied carrots and fresh green string beans with bacon and almonds. I checked the roast at the halfway mark, and it was cooking perfectly. When it was fully cooked, I removed it from the oven, removed the foil and fastened the little chef's hats on the rib bones. It was a masterpiece.

The table was set, and the food was ready at 2 pm. Rob arrived promptly, and after some initial chatting, everyone sat down at the table. The wine was poured and the salads were dished out. I made my entrance carrying the most beautiful crown roast I had ever made. I placed it on the table to amorous oohs and ahhs. Since Robbie was the guest of honor, I cut him the first rib. The knife went through the meat like butter, and I carefully laid the slice of meat on his plate and handed it back to him. He dished himself out some beans, carrots and potatoes. I proceeded to cut more slices. The smell of fresh herbs and tender pork filled the air as I continued cutting the slices. Once I had finished and everyone had a portion, I picked up my glass of wine to make a toast to my family and new friend.

I glanced over at Robbie and nearly dropped the glass from my hand. I could not believe what I saw. There, sitting in front of him, was his plate. The beautifully seasoned and perfectly cooked pork chop was

covered entirely with a good inch of thick blood-red ketchup. I wanted to scream. I wanted to march right over to him and strangle him with my bare hands. All I could do was gasp and try to regain my composure. I started my toast. "Bless all of us who are seated here today enjoying this wonderfully prepared meal and bless all of those who are less educated than us who proceed to treat a wonderfully scrumptious cut of pork like a Duraflame fireplace log." It went right over his head.

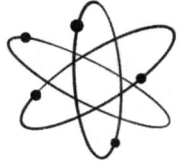

One Heck of an Ending

Why is it that some TV shows end up having substantial followers and some really good quality shows never make it past the first season, let alone a few episodes? Shows like *Friends* and *The Big Bang Theory* can go on for eight to ten seasons and command a sort of cult-like following, while other lesser-known shows like *Life in Pieces* and *The Middle* can have equally as many episodes but fade away after a while.

If you've never watched *The Middle*, you are truly missing out on some of the best family-based comedy television has ever produced.

I can relate to this really crazy offbeat and dysfunctional family, the Hecks. They lived in the middle of the country in a small town called Orson, Indiana. The dad, Mike, worked as a foreman for a local stone quarry. The mom, Frankie, had a number of jobs; but the show focused mostly on her salesperson job at a two-bit used car lot. Frankie couldn't sell a car if it were stuffed full of one-dollar bills and came with a lifetime supply of toilet paper.

Mike and Frankie had three kids. The oldest kid, Axel, was a high school teen, a typical jock with less than average brain cells who hung around with friends who were carbon copies of him. They did the typical stupid things that teens do, including getting into lots of trouble, especially when girls were involved. Axel was a slob. He drank directly from the milk carton with the fridge door wide open and walked around the house in just his boxers because he had no clean clothes, as evidenced by the piles of dirty laundry strewn all around the room he shared with his brother. He was great at football but couldn't muster a passing grade of "C" on any schoolwork assignment.

Sue, his sister, was about two years younger and was a complete mess. She had the charm and grace of a porcupine. At school, she was constantly trying out for different clubs and activities and never made any of them. Her almost sickening sweet demeanor on life was so refreshing you almost felt sorry for her with every disaster she got into. She had braces throughout most of the first few seasons, and that didn't help much with her non-existent love life. She eventually met a guy who really dug her, and they spent a lot of time together. She was smitten by him, but it took her almost four seasons to figure out he was gay.

Sue fell a lot. She must have had the worst internal gyroscope of anyone on the planet. She actually laughed off each and every misadventure as if it were just an everyday occurrence. Her perseverance was infectious.

Lastly, the youngest kid was named Brick (I'm not making that up). He was the strangest member of the family. Brick was around 10-12 years old and never grew above 4-foot-nothing. He had an unusually large head, which I'm sure was due to the insatiable amount of reading he did. He was never seen without a book nearby and was remarkably smart for his age on almost every subject. Brick also had some quirks of his own. In the early seasons, Brick would say an unusual or odd word and immediately lower his head and repeat that word in a whisper to himself. You never knew why or when he would do it.

Often, he would be in the principal's office with his parents and do his whisper thing. Eyes would roll and his parents would cover their faces in dismay. But this was just Brick. He wasn't very good at sports. Mike and Frankie would try to get the book out of his hand and force him to go outside in the yard and play. He would reluctantly saunter out, give the swing a couple of pushes and rush back into the house, stating that he did, in fact, play in the yard. Frankie would sigh, give in and hand him back his book.

Brick was really good at coming up with ways to fix all the disasters his siblings would get themselves into. He was also good at deception and cleverly brilliant at getting out of his own mischievous blunders.

The Hecks were poor. We're talking church mouse poor. If there was a poverty scale, they would be just below the lowest number. Although Mike made decent money at the quarry, he and Frankie could never make enough to get by. The washing machine door was wrapped in duct tape and occasionally walked across the room during the spin cycle. The oven was broken, so they used it to store Aunt Edie's homemade comforter. The kitchen sink leaked continuously, and buckets needed to be emptied daily. The screen door was missing glass and just hanging on by a thread. Caution had to be taken when two appliances were running at the same time because fuses would inevitably blow. Frankie tried her best to make it a happy home, but she was so busy yelling and being frustrated that a lot of that good parenting never materialized.

The reason I said that I could relate to this family is because mine was not much better. If you changed the names of the kids, changed the name of the town, and changed the jobs they did, you would have my family. Okay, I might be exaggerating a bit; but watching *The Middle* made me realize that there are some families that were worse off than ours. We lost our dad when most of us were teens. We lived paycheck to paycheck like a lot of families, and we were not much above the poverty line either.

The one thing we did have in common is that at the end of the day, we went to bed happy. We had food, shelter and lots of love. Each of us kids had his or her

quirks, too. Some of us were smart and some did not finish high school. I was great at running and gymnastics, but I could not catch a football if my life depended on it. I also had my head buried in books most of my free time. My older sisters worked various jobs and my mom worked as a maid in a nursing home. Between all of us, we pretty much lived like the Hecks, just barely making ends meet.

Unlike the Hecks, our washer worked well, the oven baked cakes and roasts, and the screen door glass broke often enough that we kept a year's supply of extra panes in the basement.

Perhaps, just like me, each one of the Hecks was also born a little atomically incorrect. Now you see why I could relate to them. We were also one HECK of a happy family.

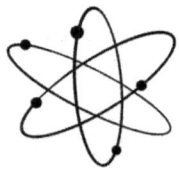

www.ingramcontent.com/pod-product-compliance
Lightning Source LLC
Chambersburg PA
CBHW071304110426
42743CB00042B/1162